Bible Devotional for Busy Families

31 Sizzling Scripture Passages *from* God's Heart

WILLIAM J. LOGE

31 Sizzling Scripture Passages from God's Heart

ISBN: 978-0-578-12353-0

Published through Believers Press/Books by the Bundle.

Printed by Bethany Press International, Bloomington, MN.

For more information visit www.FamilyBibleExperience.wordpress.com

Printed in the United States of America.
2013

Table of Contents

Acknowledgements

We live in a sinful and complex world. God spoke to my heart as I observed many young families who do not enjoy and benefit from the guidance of God's Word, the Bible. I discovered that as the Holy Spirit was leading me to write this book, He was preparing others to work alongside me with this project. My heart has been lifted with their kind words and support. These people have been vital encouragers by their prayers and God-given skills toward the completion of *31 Sizzling Scripture Passages from God's Heart*.

Thank you to all who have contributed to the vision and writing of this book:

Jamie Morrison – Executive Publisher,
Believers Press/Books by the Bundle

Bret Loge – Concept Advisor

Denise Rieke – Content Advisor

Rachel Park – Editor

Krista Fearing – Children's Book Illustrator

Stephen Henning – Landscape Painter

Becky Tighe – Artist

Dugan Design Group – Book Cover

Joy Minion – Layout/Design/Editor

Nathaniel Loge – Marketing Advisor

Jean Loge – Wife/Special Encourager/Coordinator

Plus – All who have endorsed this book

Above all: JESUS – "*Author and finisher of our faith*"
(Hebrews 12:2)

William (Bill) John Loge

Introduction

My View

God has blessed me over the years in many ways, but none as vividly and directly as through His Word, the Bible. This precious God-inspired body of truth allows the personality of the Bible writers to come through, and yet provides the very compelling message for us that God wants us to feed on daily. The Holy Scriptures bring us light with the authority we expect from the One who set in place all of creation.

Only the Bible presents a history of God working with man, spiritual insights for the listening mind, encouragement for the troubled heart, hope for the world and a divine plan for the ages. His Word points to the Savior Jesus and to His work at the cross for salvation.

Over the course of my life and my ministry years, certain passages have nearly jumped off the pages of Scripture with riveting and often delightful responses to my heart and mind. I have been led of my Lord to assemble several powerful, insightful and enjoyable passages in a book I have entitled ***31 Sizzling Passages from God's Heart***.

Important Helps

This book has been designed to provide an accommodation for families with children as well as a devotional supplement for adults. ***All of the chapters are suitable for children, but they are written with terms and expressions that give adults the opportunity to help children understand.*** For example, certain words such as "*great ovation*" in Devotional #26 are in the text and need adults to explain the meanings.

While sketches and pictures can be helpful for adults, helping children visualize Bible metaphors and characters is the primary reason for those visuals. We want those simple images to help the young capture the message of the Bible and to see the characters as real people with needs, hopes, sorrows and joys.

> If you are reading this devotional as a young family with small children, please be willing to proceed slowly if necessary, focus on the message of the Bible passage and let everybody talk about the art sketch and the connection it has to the devotional passage. Going at your own pace is important!

For the purpose of this book, the pronouns referring to God and written by the author are capitalized.

If a family wishes to go deeper than the basic devotional, note the **Extra for Adults** and **Extra for Kids** sections provided at the end of each devotional.

Occasionally there is a triangle (Δ) between paragraphs, which allows a family to break at a suitable place in the midst of a longer devotional. You may choose to place your own pause (Δ) at any point to return at a later time.

There is an **As We Pray** section at the end of each devotional. Your family may pray for those items. Note the extra number—it is an invitation for you to list your own prayer(s).

A **Devotional Reader's Guide** (page 154) provides information about devotional length, suitable break places and other items, including the date you read each devotional.

It is my prayer that you enjoy the ***31 Sizzling Scripture Passages from God's Heart*** and are touched by the wealth of the Word with this devotional. May we also be more closely conformed to the image of His Son Jesus Christ.

God Bless!
William (Bill) John Loge

1

He Never Prophesies Any Good Thing About Me!

"But Jehoshaphat asked, 'Is there not a prophet of the Lord here whom we can inquire of?' The king of Israel answered Jehoshaphat, 'There is still one man through whom we can inquire of the Lord, but I hate him because he never prophesies anything good about me, but always bad. He is Micaiah son of Imlah.'"

— 1 Kings 22:7,8

For a fuller understanding of this event, read this interesting account about two kings in consultation in 1 Kings 22:1-40. King Ahab of Israel was making his best case to Judah's King Jehoshaphat that the two nations should join to defeat the kingdom of Aram and recover control over a town called Ramoth Gilead. All the information he could secure from his 400 false prophets and advisors pointed to a decisive victory for the two nations. King Jehoshaphat was for a moment more cautious, suggesting they should make inquiry of a prophet of the Lord (verse seven).

King Ahab was quick to say there was such a man, but he hated that prophet because he never prophesied anything but trouble for him. Quite honestly I laughed at Ahab's complaint, his whining and childish response. This king had ignored the God-given Book of the Law and the enabler of Israel itself, the Lord God. He trampled without mercy on his own people, stealing from them, murdering whom he wished and leading them in Baal worship, which was strictly forbidden by the Law of Moses. He was the most evil king Israel ever had (1 Kings 6:33).

As King Ahab made his case to go to war, he complained about one of the great surviving prophets of Israel, Micaiah, who spoke true messages given to him by God. At that moment King Ahab was saying, "I want what I want. That is all I care about, and I'm going to get what I want!"

I think to some extent most of us have at one time really pushed, pulled, arranged and put aside good judgment, going ahead to obtain some big ticket item for which we have not seriously consulted the Lord. Perhaps it was a large purchase or securing a job. Without much thought and prayer we may have gone ahead with a big move for the family. We wanted it so badly that we rationalized our way to action. Often kids have pushed so hard for a toy, gift or pet that, without listening to thoughtful adults, the experience afterward became a disappointing one. King Ahab pushed hard for this war and for the kingdom of Judah to help him; and while he got what he wanted, the results were disastrous. The battle was lost, and many died. Sadly, sometimes our ill-advised decisions end up hurting others as well.

Let's note verses that help us to understand that good counsel sometimes is a healthy warning for us:

Proverbs 27:5 – "*Better is open rebuke than hidden love.*"

Ecclesiastes 7:5 – "*It is better to heed a wise man's rebuke than to listen to the song of fools.*"

Hebrews 12:5 – "*My son, do not make light of the Lord's discipline, and do not lose heart when He rebukes you.*"

Revelation 3:19 – "*Those whom I love I rebuke and discipline. So be earnest and repent.*"

Let's be thoughtful and appreciative when God's Word counsels us with a warning. It could be a lifesaver!

Extra for Adults

Deepen your understanding of the character of Ahab. Read 1 Kings 21:25-29. Is this account surprising to you? Consider Romans 9:22 and 2 Peter 3:9.

Extra for Kids

Have you ever wanted something so badly, and were disappointed when you got it? Discuss how you felt and what you did.

Why do they say owls are wise? Are they? You could look at an encyclopedia or the internet to see how smart they are.

Look up and read James 1:5. If we ask, God will give us wisdom!

As We Pray

1. Ask God to *forgive* us for times we have run ahead with an important life issue, all the while forgetting to talk to Him about it.

2. Ask for *wisdom* since God promises we can have the marvelous guidance of the One who knows us best.

3. Ask Him for *understanding* and *peace* when God somehow speaks to us that we should not go forward with what seemed at first like a good idea.

4. Your own prayer(s):

2

Sometimes Children Know Best

"If only my master would see the prophet."
— 2 Kings 5:3

Naaman commanded the army of the King of Aram. In many ways he was successful. Naaman was held in high regard by the King of Aram because of his many military victories. He had recently raided Israel and took away as captive a little Israelite girl, whom he gave as a servant to his wife. Enjoy reading 2 Kings 5:1-19a for the intriguing account.

The problem mostly on Naaman's mind was that he had been stricken with leprosy. Leviticus chapter 13 shows the seriousness of this disease: it destroyed flesh, was contagious and was eventually fatal. It seems Naaman had either a mild variant of the disease or was in the early stages of the dreaded affliction. Separation from society was a further blow to this proud man.

The young enslaved girl played a part in the dilemma. She could have been the invisible person in this drama, but instead she stepped forward with good advice. She was in fact a key person in God's plan. She implored her mistress to have Naaman seek the prophet Elisha for healing of his illness. Her upbringing in Israel reminded her of the prophet Elisha, who spoke for the true God of Israel. She was unwillingly taken from her home in Israel as a captive, separated from her homeland and her family. When she said, "*I wish my master would go to see the prophet in Samaria*" (2 Kings 5:3 *NLT*), she did not appear bitter but full of compassion for her master. Bad experiences, whatever they were, did not leave her useless in respect to being a servant girl or pointing her owners to God's prophet, Elisha. Her attitude is a lesson for us to be caring servants of God despite unhappy circumstances.

Follow the "people trail" with me to the healing of Naaman:

Servant Girl *(start here)*

Mistress

Naaman

King

Elisha

Elisha's Messenger

Naaman's Officer

Healing of Naaman

It all started with the young servant girl! The young maid's name is not even mentioned, but she was the one who got things going in the right direction.

Do you ever feel that your words pointing others to Jesus as Savior don't mean that much? They do. Even if no results are immediately visible, your testimony makes a difference!

Extra for Adults

Do you think the servant girl exercised faith? If Naaman had not found Elisha or if he had not taken Elisha's advice, could things have become difficult for her?

Children, like adults, can make bad decisions that hurt others around them. Look at 2 Kings 2:23-24: rather than honor Elisha, the boys got into big trouble taunting him. That episode ended in disaster. Proverbs 20:11 says, "*Even a child is known by his actions, by whether his conduct is pure and right.*"

Let's respect children. We need to affirm them when they choose to do what's right. Let's pray for them to make good decisions.

Extra for Kids

Are you familiar with the account of the feeding of the 5,000 in John 6:1-15? Notice how it was a boy who offered the food he had. What food did he offer Jesus? This willing boy provided the small lunch, and Jesus gave thanks for that food (verse 11).

Hey, kids, God will use you for really good things as you trust and live for Him. God bless as you go to it!

As We Pray

1. Thank God for all the Bible accounts that tell about children and their great value. Thank Him for the children in your family.

2. Pray that children in your neighborhood and at church will become believers in Jesus if they are not. Pray for them by name.

3. Pray for parents and adults that they may have wisdom, understanding, love and patience with children they look after. Pray for them by name.

4. Your own prayer(s):

3

Lying to Be Rich? No Problem

"'Everything is all right,' Gehazi answered. 'My master sent me to say,' "Two young men from the company of the prophets have just come to me from the hill country of Ephraim. Please give them a talent of silver and two sets of clothing"' ... Then he went in and stood before his master Elisha. 'Where have you been, Gehazi?' Elisha asked. 'Your servant didn't go anywhere,' Gehazi answered."

— 2 Kings 5:22, 25

In this account Gehazi lied twice. Read the full account in 2 Kings 5:16-27.

Ever wonder how great and beautiful things sometimes are followed by ugly things? In this passage Naaman, the Aram commander, was healed of his leprosy, a terrible skin disease. When the prophet Elisha was offered many gifts to be placed on mules for him to take, listen to Elisha's response: "*As surely as the Lord lives, whom I serve, I will not accept a thing*"(verse 16). Surely the commander was impressed with Elisha's unselfishness!

The thought of having all that stuff Elisha turned down was too much for Gehazi, and he set out to get those things for himself. Naaman felt joy in the victory of God's healing, but greed got the best of Gehazi. He carried out his plot to deceive Elisha. He stole, lied and demonstrated contempt for Elisha and his instructions in the midst of an otherwise joyous event.

Gehazi most certainly never anticipated the consequences of his sins, which were uglier than the original leprosy of Naaman. As a result, Gehazi was given the leprosy of Naaman, and the disease would even follow through to his descendants. Because of these acts, Gehazi was removed from the presence of Elisha (verse 27). The good news of Naaman's healing was followed by a sad chapter for Gehazi and those around him.

Good news and blessings were abounding with the beginning of the church. The early church believers were "*one in heart and mind*" (Acts 4:32) when Satan led Ananias and Sapphira in a plan to deceive the church with their dishonesty. They wished for recognition for a gift they had not fully given, so they lied. Death came to this couple, while grief and fear came to the church (Acts 5:1ff).

When good and blessed events happen around us, let's be aware of the potential of Satan's temptations and of our human weakness. Let's not move from God and bring dishonor and harm upon ourselves and those near us.

In our personal and church life, even the joy of someone converted to Christ, the excitement of a building program or a generous gift can be followed by a sad happening. The Apostle Peter said we need to be alert, warning believers of Satan's work to take us away from faith and godliness (1 Peter 5:8).

Extra for Adults

How many outright lies did Satan put before Jesus in Matthew 4:1-11? How did Satan use pieces of truth in his attempt to lead Jesus astray? Are we on guard for Satan's craftiness to do the same to us?

Extra for Kids

1. How have you felt when you are caught lying?
2. Will lying help you? Find and read Proverbs 19:5.
3. Will God forgive us for lying? See 1 John 1:9, and mark it in your Bible.

As We Pray

Suggested prayers:

1. "Lord, forgive me of my sins."
2. "Lord, help me to be alert to avoid deceit when something is not quite right or is dishonest with my business, with You or any person."
3. "May my reputation be so honest that people within the church and outside the church will praise God because of my truthful character."
4. Your own prayer(s):

"I know that my Redeemer lives, and that in the end he will stand upon the earth." —Job 19:25

4

The Killing Machine

"'Don't be afraid,' the prophet answered. 'Those who are with us are more than those who are with them.'"

— 2 Kings 6:16

Chariots go back a long way. Historians found them in use in about 2000 B.C. Ancient chariots were usually two-wheeled wagons pulled by one or two horses and could accommodate from one to three people. Originally, the chariots seemed to be used mostly for pageantry and for the transportation of important rulers. Soon after Joseph was placed in charge of the whole land of Egypt, Pharaoh celebrated by having him ride in a chariot as men shouted, "*Make way*" (Genesis 41:41,43). The better chariots had floors made of a rope network to soften the ride.

Chariots also were built and used for war. They were often equipped with special storage compartments on the side for bows, spears and arrows. The four-wheeled Aramean chariot as shown in our chariot sketch could punish ground forces. Their fierce-looking appearance was enough to frighten foot soldiers, who were often already tired from walking great distances.

When the Prophet Elisha's servant woke up one morning, he went outside and became terrified to find that the Aramean army with horses and armored chariots had surrounded them. Please read the text in 2 Kings 6:8-17.

Notice from verse 16 that Elisha had vision to see the chariots of God that the servant did not have. Elisha didn't hesitate in expressing his desire to share that view of God's protection, and he prayed God would open the eyes of the servant. Isn't it great when God's prophets, pastors and leaders want those in their care to have spiritual vision and to excel in knowing the deep things of God?

When we serve Him today, whether as teacher, pastor or parent, may the Lord keep us from holding up our religious position or status for others to admire. Like Elisha, let's have a passion in our heart that those in our care might enjoy the growth, vision and maturity that God has given us.

In my imagination, I see Elisha's servant with a big smile of relief as he sees "*the hills full of* [God's] *horses and chariots of fire all around Elisha*" (verse 17). I have seen several fascinating pictures of different chariots, even one of solid gold from Egypt. But to envision hills full of chariots of fire, let's call them "sizzling" chariots; that would beat them all!

The picture of the fiery chariots is a wonderful symbol of God's protective hand around those who are His. Psalm 34:7 says, "*The angel of the Lord encamps around those who fear him, and he delivers them.*"

While God uses angels, spiritual beings and even men to protect us, it is God Himself who assures us of our care. The Psalmist said it clearly: "*Some trust in chariots and some in horses, but we trust in the name of the Lord our God*" (Psalm 20:7).

If you ever wonder today about God's promise to watch over us, consider Hebrews 13:5: "*Never will I leave you; never will I forsake you.*" When we die, does God's promise to watch over us expire? The apostle Paul wrote, "*The Lord ... will bring me safely to His heavenly kingdom*" (2 Timothy 4:18). That's even better than chariots of fire!

> *The Lord bless you and keep you; the Lord make his face shine upon you and be gracious to you; the Lord turn his face toward you and give you peace.*
>
> – Numbers 6:24-26

Extra for Adults

Elisha's servant was somewhat like all of us. He faced fear. In this situation God allowed him to see those fiery chariots to assure him that God was there in force to protect them.

Today we have a fuller revelation of God's Word than the servant had in Elisha's time. Read Luke 12:1-7. Just think of Jesus' words to the disciples and the "*many thousands*" (verse 1) as He told them not to fear in verse four.

Jesus said, "*The very hairs of your head are all numbered*"; and while God remembers every sparrow, we are "*worth more than many sparrows*" (verse seven). Because of His love and care, sleep well tonight.

Extra for Kids

Would you like to see a chariot of **solid gold**? If you can, try searching for "chariots of King Tut's tomb" on the internet.

King Tut died at 19 years of age and was buried with much gold and jewelry. He was also buried with six chariots, some made of gold. Did that gold chariot make King Tut better off when he was buried with it? There is something better than gold, gold chariots or any chariot to keep you from being afraid.

The servant learned not to fear when he saw God's chariots—it meant God was protecting him. Because God wants to tell you how much He loves you and will protect all who trust in Him, He gave these bird-like words to the writer of Psalm 91:4 (*NLT*):

> *He will cover you with his feathers. He will shelter you with his wings. His faithful promises are your armor and protection.*

As We Pray

1. Praise God for all the promises He gave for our care and encouragement.
2. Pray that God will help us grow in our faith: Lord, help me to grow to "*live by faith, not by sight*" (2 Corinthians 5:7).
3. Pray we will see the limitless power of God and realize by faith that He knows our situation. Pray we will trust Him when facing our fears.
4. Pray we will not fear men and we will sleep well tonight.
5. Your own prayer(s):

5

How About Killing Them? No, Let's Feed Them!

Which is it?

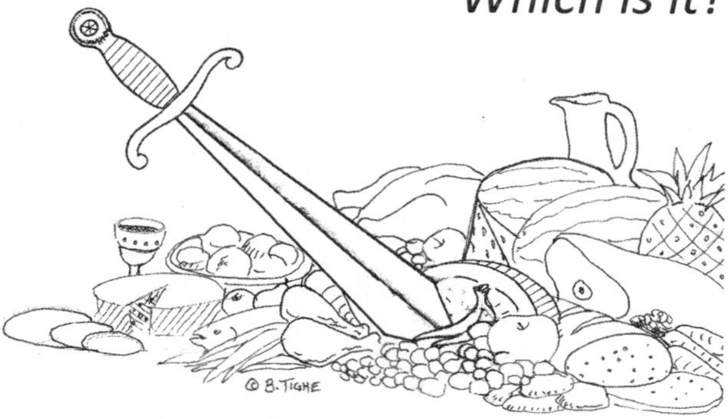

"When the King of Israel saw them, he asked Elisha, 'Shall I kill them, my father? Shall I kill them?' 'Do not kill them ... Set food and water before them so that they may eat and drink and then go back to their master.'"

— 2 Kings 6:21, 22

For a fuller text, read 2 Kings 6:18-23.

Let's look at two of the real life players involved in this feast for enemy soldiers before considering this dramatic event. The date is about 892 B.C., and Israel's King Ahab and his son Ahaziah had died. The succeeding King Jehoram, a brother of Ahaziah, took the throne of Israel; while removing Baal worship in the kingdom, he still permitted and practiced idolatry.

King Jehoram once wore sackcloth under his robes, which normally signified heavy affliction and mourning (6:30). However, in the years of Jehoram's reign there was little evidence of the king's faith in God or a surrendered heart. One scholar of Old Testament kings described Jehoram's heart this way: (Jehoram had) "no surrender of the heart and the will to God ... His repentance was but a half-repentance."[1] Without being firmly rooted in trusting God, the absence of spiritual depth left this ruler inconsistent and weak. Surprisingly, the same King Jehoram who called out to Elisha as "*father*" later called for his beheading! (See verses 21, 31.)

While Jehoram was a model of inconsistency, Elisha was one of steadiness in the Lord. When under pressure, the prophet Elisha kept his eyes on God and walked in obedience to Him.

The big feast came about this way: despite a spiritually weak king and nation, God answered Elisha's prayer that the Aramean army would be struck with blindness. Surely this miracle was met with great relief and gladness by King Jehoram and his people. The dangerous enemy was duped into marching right into the capital of Israel. Aram's army was completely at the mercy of the opposition as their eyes were opened inside Israel's capital city, Samaria. Once within the fortified capital, they were face to face with Israel's people, soldiers and the unpredictable King Jehoram. Savor this predicament for a moment!

The account records fairly complex events considering it is but six verses in length. Allow me to highlight some of the history and drama of this event, which leads me to note some humor as well as a serious application.

Think about the setting of the captured enemy forces in Samaria. Consider the king and the Israelite soldiers ready for brutal action. Imagine the stares and glares from Samaritan city dwellers upon their trapped foes! While King Jehoram proposed slaughtering them, Elisha called for the king to not kill but provide food and water for them. What did the king do? Not satisfied with just feeding the enemy soldiers a simple meal, we read, "*He prepared a great feast for them; and after they had finished eating and drinking, he sent them away*" (verse 23). Israel's feasts often included roasted lamb or boiled beef, wheat and barley breads, grapes, olives, figs, pomegranates, lentils and grape juice or wine. After the great feast the spared soldiers went home. What relief came to those soldiers who at one time thought they were "cooked goose," and then they were served "cooked goose"! Think about Romans 12:20-21, which says: "*If your enemy is hungry, feed him; .... Do not be overcome by evil, but overcome evil with good.*"

Δ

This drama of 2 Kings 6:18-23 records the people of Israel giving a feast to enemy soldiers. It has four major human points of view, each of them with intriguing segments that rival any recent movie release!

The ***first*** of these was **King Jehoram**, who had nothing to do with the subduing of the Aramean army. Upon witnessing the favorable events that trapped the feared enemy inside Israel's walls, the first thing the king thought was to orchestrate a great slaughter. King Jehoram made the remarkable proposition, "*Shall I kill them, my father? Shall I kill them?*" (verse 21).

Jehoram's unbelief toward God, frequent hate for Elisha and resistance of Elisha's counsel marked Jehoram's eight-year rule. In some ways his life was particularly tragic because of the many times he was able to see God work through Elisha and how the great prophet appealed to this king. The ending summary of Jehoram's life? "*He did evil in the eyes of the LORD*" (2 Kings 8:18).

The ***second*** point of view was that of **Elisha**. One who lived knowing young Elisha as an aggressive farmer would also know his heart for God, his trust in God and his fervent desire to serve Him. His bold prayer was that the enemy be stricken with blindness, that Israel would again be delivered and that the people would see they must trust in God!

Elisha's prayer was answered, and the enemy was blinded. The drama did not end with an incapacitated Aramean army. Elisha had other thoughts in order to deliver Israel. He summoned the clueless foe to follow him (verse 19). Elisha became the point man in this long procession to Samaria, the Israel capital. I wonder how the guards at the city walls responded as Elisha and the blind enemy soldiers came to the city gates. This remarkable procession led by Elisha trekked right into the city of Samaria. Then they had their eyes opened.

When Jehoram called for the prisoners' slaughter, Elisha chastised him:

> *Do not kill them.... Would you kill men you have captured with your own sword or bow? Set food and water before them so that they may eat and drink and then go back to their master.* — 2 Kings 6:22

While Elisha drew attention to an often ignored, ancient code of civil behavior toward captive people, the king was poised with a solution to kill. Elisha is a powerful example of how one person of God can set and lead many people to behave with a higher moral standard.

In Titus 2:7 we read, "*In everything set them an example by doing what is good.*" Can you think of someone who has been an example to you? How might we take a stand that would encourage others to behave with a higher moral standard?

Δ

The ***third*** human point of view was from the **Aramean soldiers**. The experience in Samaria certainly gave the once-trapped warriors something to tell their families about when they got home! Notice that the bands stopped raiding Israel's territory (verse 23). War returned eventually, but the captives set free wouldn't have forgotten their experience.

The beginning of their fateful experience began as they gathered their weapons, chariots and horses. Under the orders of the Aramean king, this robust army set out to capture Elisha at Dothan (2 Kings 6:13). Blinded and duped, they followed Elisha into Samaria and were certainly terrified. Their future looked dim as the Israelite king seemed to urge they be killed. They would never forget the feast after their near death.

Let's be mindful of this as we consider the ***fourth*** point of view was the **people of Israel**. Not all of Israel were people of faith. In fact, often the majority were not. But God still revealed Himself and His standards to them. The people of Israel are a chosen nation for God's purpose. People of God find it gratifying to see the forces of God win over the forces of evil, and we are thankful. But God brings us something more than just our victories. G. Rawlinson wrote,

> Elisha showed the king of Israel "a more excellent way." Here surely in the Old Testament, breathes the spirit of the New. It is Christ's precept of doing good to enemies, of returning good for evil, of seeking to overcome evil with good.[2]

The people of Israel were known to take in foreigners and aliens who would worship the God of Israel. But how would God communicate His love and grace to a large detachment of enemy soldiers, who were basically prisoners in Israel? The feast and freedom of the enemy was God's grace at work!

I see this passage as a special glimpse of God's grace. Other Old Testament saints had the view toward returning good for evil, as the teacher of the Proverbs wrote: "*If your enemy is hungry, give him food to eat; if he is thirsty, give him water to drink*" (Proverbs 25:21).

2 Kings 6 has all the characters and drama of a great play. But we are more than actors; we are real people, who have influence on those around us. Be encouraged as you see the example of Elisha as a man faithful to God, who often stood alone and led courageously while serving the Lord, yet who showed a tender side of his personality. We, too, can have a positive influence on many around us.

Do you have unfriendly people in your world each day or with whom you feel a strong indifference? You might try a feast, or just doing something nice toward those people in your life who oppose you. They could change, and you will be blessed as you love them in Jesus' name! Think about this verse: "*Those who are wise will shine like the brightness of the heavens, and those who lead many to righteousness, like the stars for ever and ever*" (Daniel 12:3).

If you are impressed with the patience and character of Elisha but you have not trusted God as your Savior, would you read the "Steps to Peace with God" in the back of this book? It was God's love and patience that worked through this dramatic event. The "Steps" will help you see that God loves and cares for you, and you can know God personally.

Extra for Adults

Remember the Bible story of the officer in charge of the gate that got trampled? It was under King Jehoram's rule, and the passage is 2 Kings 6:24-7:20. It will take about ten minutes to read. You will see a demonstration of anger, good news, conscience, unbelief and judgment. You will also see examples of good character and bad character greatly affecting the lives of others.

Extra for Kids

Two things to color:

1. Can you color or draw a picture of several angry looking enemy soldiers, horses and chariots on hills like 2 Kings 6:14, 15 describes? Make the soldiers **black**.

2. Then go to verse 17, color or draw even many "more" of God's horses and chariots, but do them in **red**. Don't worry if you have a hard time drawing horses. (I am terrible at drawing horses.) An important thing is to use a big piece of paper or tape two or three pieces together. When you are done, that is a picture of God's power to help us!

As We Pray

1. Thank God for all the prophets and godly people who point us to God.

2. Thank God for the Bible.

3. Ask the Lord to help us see how He works today, changes people and does miracles.

4. Your own prayer(s):

[1] G. Rawlinson. *The Pulpit Commentary on II Kings,* Vol. 5. Grand Rapids: Eerdmans (1978), 128.

[2] Ibid.

"*Submit yourselves, then, to God. Resist the devil, and he will flee from you.*"
— James 4:7

6

Bare Bones Bring Body Back

"Elisha died and was buried. Now Moabite raiders used to enter the country every spring. Once while some Israelites were burying a man, suddenly they saw a band of raiders; so they threw the man's body into Elisha's tomb. When the body touched Elisha's bones, the **[dead]** ***man came to life and stood up on his feet."***

— 2 Kings 13:20, 21

Put yourself in the Israelites' shoes. They were in the middle of performing a sobering task: the burial of a fellow Israelite. A band of Moabite raiders appeared nearby, and they became very frightened. Facing this danger they had to move quickly; they apparently put off any sense of ceremony, and as the text says, "*threw*" the body into Elisha's tomb. With fear at the approaching soldiers, they probably gasped and stared in amazement as the dead man's body touched the bones of the long-dead prophet, came alive and stood up. I expect the fear level of that burial party multiplied at that moment.

Perhaps this was a serious moment, but I confess I have a big chuckle every time I read it. This was a real life experience for this little group of Israelites that likely was told many times over; I'm sure it was very entertaining for both tellers and listeners!

What do we make of this passage, and how can we apply it to our lives? What made the body of the dead man come alive when it touched Elisha's bones? Clearly it was the life-giving power of the Creator God, whom Elisha worshipped. God had used Elisha to pray over a lifeless boy, resulting in the child coming back to life (2 Kings 4:32-37). Elisha was a great prophet who trusted God for miracles; and though Elisha was dead, his good influence continued—even in the grave!

The same God, who brought life to the dead Israelite, works to give life to us today!

Do you know that he who believes in Christ has "*everlasting life*" (John 6:47)? If you have not believed by acknowledging Jesus as God's Son, repented of your sin and placed your faith in Him as your Savior, won't you do that now? If you are unsure if you have everlasting life, "Steps to Peace with God," which is in the back of this book, can help you find this hope in Christ.

Extra for Adults

The context around Elisha's ministry is marked by calling on God for preserving life and providing food. We often think of the times Jesus worked miracles to provide faint crowds with good food. Isn't it interesting that 900 years before Christ God miraculously fed 100 people—and there were leftovers? Read 2 Kings 4:42-44. You may be intrigued by all the food and water references in Elisha's ministry from 2 Kings 2:19 through 7:20.

Extra for Kids

1. If we know Jesus as our Savior, we know we have everlasting life. Do you know the verse John 3:16? If not, look it up.

2. Knowing we believers will be with Jesus in heaven some day when we die is a great promise. But that doesn't make it any easier when someone close to us dies, just like when a child died in Elisha's time. Read 2 kings 4:32-37, where Elisha has a part in bringing this boy to life. Whom does he ask for help? What else does he do? We will have tears, but we must go to God for comfort and help like Elisha did.

As We Pray

1. Thank God for His creation of life. Thank Him for the victory over death that He provides. We are "*passed from death unto life*" (John 5:24 *KJV*).

2. Pray that others would see the life and hope in us that comes from knowing Jesus and that they would be drawn to Him.

3. Your own prayer(s):

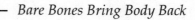

"*Give, and it will be given to you. A good measure, pressed down, shaken together and running over, will be poured into your lap. For with the measure you use, it will be measured to you.*" – Luke 6:38

7

God's Word ... Stored in the Temple or Stored in the Heart?

"When the king heard the words of the Law, he tore his robes.... 'Because your heart was responsive and you humbled yourself before God when you heard what he spoke against this place and its people, and because you humbled yourself before me and tore your robes and wept in my presence, I have heard you,' declares the Lord."

— 2 Chronicles 34:19, 27

A fuller text is 2 Chronicles 34:1, 2, 14-28.

Throughout the history of the ancient kingdoms of Judah and Israel, there were good kings and bad. Leading up to King

Josiah's reign of Judah in about 634 B.C., there had been ruling kings who led the two countries away from worshipping the true God of their fathers. Instead they worshipped idols and embraced many forms of sinful behavior. The Book of the Law of the LORD given through Moses was stored in the temple and was but a faint memory. Without God's guiding Word, both Judah and Israel were in trouble internally and externally with other nations.

Josiah became king at eight years of age; when he was 16, he began to earnestly seek God and to destroy the idols that had been put in God's place. King Josiah continued as a religious reformer. When several years later the Book of the Law from the temple was brought out to him and read in his presence, the king was deeply moved and tore his garments. Tearing one's robes in ancient times was a visible expression of intense grief.

King Josiah assembled a large group of leaders and citizens and read the Book of the Covenant to them. The king and the people pledged to follow the teachings of God's Word. That public reading renewed awareness of God's desire that the people worship Him only, and their confession of sin brought about remarkable changes. God was pleased as they pledged themselves to Him. Despite judgment to come, the nation of Israel was far better off when the Word of God was brought out from obscurity. The same is true for us today: "*Your word is a lamp to my feet and a light for my path*" (Psalm 119:105).

During the U.S. Civil War, Thomas Jonathan "Stonewall" Jackson led the outnumbered Confederate army to three remarkable battle victories near Harrisonburg, Virginia. The Union side chose Colonel Philip Sheridan to lead the Union army. Sheridan set out to defeat the southern army by stripping away the resources of the rich Shenandoah Valley. Billows of smoke gave vivid evidence of burning barns, homes, crops and factories, which had provided food for the south, leaving the soldiers hungry, weak and in some cases starving.

We starve ourselves in our Christian pilgrimage without the fresh resource of the Bible in our lives. Not having this spiritual food daily robs us of our spiritual, emotional and even intellectual strength for the demands before us. Stripped of the knowledge of God's moral absolutes and plans, we are uninformed of God's will and spiritually malnourished. We become weak in our Christian walk. "*I have hidden your word in my heart that I might not sin against you,*" the Psalmist wrote in Psalm 119:11.

We have a choice. Let's not allow ourselves to become weak by ignoring His Word. Be like Josiah: give prominence to reading and applying God's Word. Instead of becoming stripped of the nourishment, we need to fruitfully live our lives in Christ. Our reading of the Word shows God that we have an awareness of its great value. "*I rejoice in your word, like one who discovers a great treasure*" (Psalm 119:162 *NLT*). Why not decide this day to be enthused and regular in reading God's Word, the Bible, daily?

Extra for Adults

1. Read 2 Chronicles 34:8-33.
2. How were some Israelites affected adversely by Josiah's reforms?
3. How did the Lord respond to Josiah's leadership and humility?
4. What plans of God were not to change?
5. Do you see parallels from this passage to your own country?

Extra for Kids

1. How would you like to have been an eight-year-old king like Josiah was, or an eight-year-old queen? Would it be hard if older folks gave you advice?

2. Josiah made big decisions. Help me list things kids can decide to do that please God.
   a. Be cheerful.
   b. Be happy to help with chores.
   c. Pray for family.
   d.
   e.
   f.

As We Pray

1. Pray that God will help us to read His Word each day and hide it in our hearts.

2. Pray that He would help us to obey His Word.

3. Pray for our church to read the Word publically and study it with all ages.

4. Your own prayer(s):

8

Fox Alert: "Fox Likely to Topple New Wall!"

***"That stone wall would collapse if even a fox walked along the top of it!"* (Tobiah)**

— Nehemiah 4:3 (*NLT*)

***"The wall was finished—just fifty-two days after we had begun. When our enemies and the surrounding nations heard about it, they were frightened and humiliated. They realized this work had been done with the help of our God."* (Possibly Nehemiah)**

— Nehemiah 6:15, 16 (*NLT*)

Nehemiah, a contrite man of God, was also a man of faith and vision. After acquiring Persian King Artaxeres' permission, blessing and support, Nehemiah set out from serving as the king's cupbearer to rebuilding the city of Jerusalem. Read the remarkable account of Nehemiah 1:1 - 2:10.

Nehemiah's project was more than the engineering and rebuilding of 2½ miles of broken down walls and principal buildings. One of the greatest challenges was to lead a small group of Jerusalem survivors, who were hurting from years of suppression and physical abuse.

Sanballat, a local official, suggested Nehemiah was rebelling against the king (2:19); he later mocked Nehemiah's builders saying, "*Can they bring the stones back to life from those heaps of rubble – burned as they are?*" (4:2). Another one of the abusers was Tobiah, the Ammonite who heaped ridicule on the builders declaring, "*That stone wall would collapse if even a fox walked along the top of it*" (4:3 *NLT*).

When Secretary of State William H. Seward had a dream to increase the United States geographically by 20% and to purchase Alaska for approximately two cents an acre, he was constantly ridiculed. Political opponents called Alaska "Seward's Icebox" and "President Andrew Johnson's Polar Bear Garden." Because of political moves, the purchase was actually not funded until a year after the treaty was signed – and even then Congress passed the purchase by only a one-vote margin. The detractors continued, saying that the President just wanted another appointment – in this case "Superintendent of Walruses." Seward and Johnson were desperately trying to lift the hearts of Americans suffering from years of hurt and disunity caused by the Civil War, which had just ended. Yet consider the significance: the $7.2 million purchase of Alaska, which has richly blessed U.S. citizens.

In our walk with Christ, our intentions to show love to our neighbor, to involve ourselves in a missions trip or even to give to a Christian cause will often result in cutting remarks and ridicule. These can result in harsh and unfair things being said as we have acted on our Christian convictions.

I have a friend who donated a large tract of land to an evangelistic ministry. This gift was met with scorn by many. Someone wrote in the local newspaper that what he called "giving to the 'church' chunks of land" was detrimental to the community and would deprive many of needed funds that would be lost from the tax base. Being a good neighbor, this deeply hurt my friend; yet with the affirmation of Christian brothers, he stayed the course and completed the gift.

Ridicule can cut deeply in the hearts of those with big dreams and good motives. As believers, we must stay true to the vision of ministry God has given us! God will help us. "*Do not be overcome by evil, but overcome evil with good*" (Romans 12:21).

Δ

Words can hurt deeply. Proverbs 15:4 says, "*The tongue that brings healing is a tree of life, but a deceitful tongue crushes the spirit.*" If you should be hurt or even demoralized by words, try the example of Nehemiah.

The ***first*** thing Nehemiah did when he was stung by constant ridicule was to **call on God**: "*Hear us, O our God, for we are despised. Turn their insults back on their own heads*" (Nehemiah 4:4). When Jesus gave His followers a model prayer, He instructed them to pray to "*deliver us from evil*" (Matthew 6:13 *KJV*). Each of us needs to call on the Lord as we take hurting words seriously. Ask Him to help us to be delivered from those poisonous darts.

As Nehemiah labored on, the text says that the people's strength was "*giving out*" (Nehemiah 4:10). This bold leader knew he must **encourage the laborers**. The ***second*** thing he did was to stand up among the leaders and all the people and say, "*Don't be afraid of them. Remember the Lord, who is great and* *awesome, and fight for your brothers, your sons and your daughters, your wives and your homes*" (4:14).

The writer of Hebrews instructed us to "*encourage one another daily*" (Hebrews 3:13). If we are hurting from the verbal stings from the world, we can be sure that other brothers and sisters are, too! Let's keep our antennas up, being quick to step up to our fellow believers and comfort them, always pointing them to our awesome God and His help.

The ***third*** thing we see that Nehemiah did was to **get back to work**. For him and the people of Judah, it was to fight for family (4:14); return to the wall—the task God had led them to in 4:15; work hard and be vigilant at the same time (4:17); and protect each other (4:22, 23). Nehemiah had led the people to apply the message of Psalm 100:2 (*KJV*): "*Serve the Lord with gladness.*"

The bottom line is this: as you serve the Lord and if anyone says that a fox could cause your wall to tumble, you may think how that is silly. Take stinging words right to the Lord in prayer. Call on Him to lift you up! Let His Spirit comfort you. Then encourage those around you who are in the faith. They are precious to God, and He wants you to encourage them. Get back to work! Build your wall as He leads. Be diligent and joyful in serving Him. You will be blessed.

Extra for Adults

Notice how many times Nehemiah burst out in prayer in Nehemiah 1-6. Find the verses yourself, or check out 1:4; 2:4; 4:4, 9; 5:13, 19; 6:9, 14. Nehemiah was a man of prayer! Wouldn't he be neat to have as a Christian friend?

Nehemiah comes across as a reverent and thoughtful man, yet he was a "bundle of energy"! Perhaps if we served with such a person as him, we would be very stretched—but that would be good for us. Nehemiah was a remarkable example of one trusting and serving God with his countrymen of 445 B.C. He is that for us today, too!

Extra for Kids

1. Look at Nehemiah 4:16-18. How many different groups of people do you find? Which job would you like the best?
2. Why do you think they didn't change clothes (4:23)? What did they take with them when they got water?
3. Like Nehemiah, have you ever had people around you who just don't want to be friends? Maybe they do bad stuff and get you into trouble? Talk to God about it. Talk to a good friend who loves Jesus. God will help you, and then you can help others. Keep following Jesus!

As We Pray

1. Pray that we will handle bad words directed at us by praying, encouraging others and getting back to work.

2. Pray that we will know what "our wall" might be, such as a big task we feel God wants us to do. It may be pleasing parents, showing God's love at school/at work/to neighbors, helping the pastor, starting a Bible study, stepping out to a foreign mission field or something else God has placed in your heart.

3. Ask God to help give you a good-thinking mind, energy and victory over evil voices.

4. Your own prayer(s):

"He who overcomes will, like them, be dressed in white. I will never blot out his name from the book of life, but will acknowledge his name before my Father and his angels." – Revelation 3:5

9

Lord, I Feel Kind of Small at the Moment

"When I look up into the night skies and see the work of your fingers—the moon and the stars you have made—I cannot understand how you can bother with mere puny man, to pay any attention to him!"

— Psalm 8:3, 4 (*TLB*)

This paraphrase captures my own sense of wonderment about why a sovereign God would go to such lengths to reach out to us as humans. A big part of the reason is that we were made in His image (Genesis 1:26). Our mind, will, emotions, self-consciousness and even our human desire to create and to solve problems are after God's likeness, even though we are spiritually fallen creatures. You can see the fuller text in Psalm 8:1-9.

Every July 4th Americans celebrate the founding of our country. I'm amused every year in hearing the expected oohs and aahs from admirers as the sky is lit up with colored fireworks. To think that the great heavens outside our door are but a small part of God's creation is mind-boggling. As you see the vast, bright span of stars in their consistent places in the evening skies, you may feel the urge to pray as David in Psalm 8:4, "*What is man that you are mindful of him?*"

You may be alone or with others, but I have a challenge for you. When it is dark, get a flashlight and a Bible. Go out on your front steps or your back porch. You may have to bundle up or slather on bug repellent, but it will be worth it! Gaze up at the stars and enjoy thinking of God, Creator of the heavenly expanse. Read Psalm 8:3-4, look to heaven and sing the Doxology or substitute any song of praise or worship. If you're not cold or eaten by mosquitoes, linger outside awhile. Looking to the heaven, talk to Him. Thank Him for creation's beauty and His love. Tell Him your impression of the sky above.

Whether indoors or out and if you have extra time, look at some verses that speak of God's incredible being and His love toward us:

Psalm 19:1-6 – The heavens declare God's glory.

Romans 8:35 – Nothing separates us from God's love.

2 Peter 3:9 – He is patient with you.

Extra for Adults

Psalm 8 sets forth a paradox. Our God, who has created beyond our comprehension, is the same God who speaks through the Word that we are of great value. While He will bring judgment to all who resist Him, consider the Apostle

Paul's words, "*But God demonstrates his own love for us in this: While we were still sinners; Christ died for us*" (Romans 5:8). Join those who look into the sky and say, "Thank You for paying attention to me!"

Extra for Kids

1. Did you know that Jesus was known as a Star? See Revelation 22:16.

2. Do you know that you can be like a star? See Philippians 2:14-15.

As We Pray

1. Thank Him for creation and its beauty, for good things we enjoy and for Jesus.

2. Praise Him for reaching out to us by sending a Savior.

3. Pray that we will be pure and shine like a star.

4. Ask Him to help us with problems we have like school, work, and/or illness.

5. Your own prayer(s):

"If my people, who are called by my name, will humble themselves and pray and seek my face and turn from their wicked ways, then will I hear from heaven and will forgive their sin and will heal their land." – 2 Chronicles 7:14

10

The Incredible Super Talkers

"Too much talk leads to sin. Be sensible and keep your mouth shut."

— Proverbs 10:19 (*NLT*)

Once a very busy lady invited some guests for dinner. Wanting to please her company, she planned a large meal and discovered she was short of several items she had counted on. Just in time, however, everything came together, the full course meal was set and she regained her composure in time to welcome her friends.

Soon everyone was at the table and ready for what was obviously the result of a lot of effort. Turning with pride to her six-year-old daughter and helper, she asked if she would say the blessing.

"I don't know what to say," the little girl replied.

"Just say what you hear Mommy say," the hostess said.

The daughter bowed her head and said, "**Lord, why on earth did I invite all these people to dinner!**"

I think all of us from time to time say things we wish could be taken back. Sometimes we regret it most when we are quoted! The Word of God has a lot to say about our speech.

Proverbs 10:19 is blunt, but true: "*Too much talk leads to sin.*" Some of us just talk too much! Occasionally we meet actual "super talkers," who loudly dominate group conversations and are guilty of the sin of pride as they shut out others from offering their opinions and thoughts.

I think we should exempt "super talkers" under the age of three. The little chatterboxes are just trying out new equipment! But at some point they, too, need to learn to listen and talk nice as they are led by godly adults.

Solomon and James both spoke to the issue of too many words leading to serious spiritual issues. The Apostle James told us, "*If anyone considers himself religious and yet does not keep a tight rein on his tongue, he deceives himself and his religion is worthless*" (James 1:26). That's pretty strong medicine!

I think that when we talk excessively somehow unguarded words creep into our comments. The Apostle Paul spoke of his spiritual warfare: "*I love God's law with all my heart. But there is another power within me that is at war with my mind*" (Romans 7:22, 23 *NLT*). An unbridled tongue can give opportunity to sin. Let's be careful in what we say and the volume of words that come out!

Some of us feel we just have so much to say. There are times when quieter people have difficulty expressing themselves when asked even a simple question. It is fair to acknowledge that some folks speak well, and others seem by nature to be very quiet.

I attended a 50th wedding anniversary celebration, and toward the end of a program the attentive but silent husband was asked to say something. His only words were, "I've said too much already!"

We don't want to sidestep God's sizzling counsel to us: "*Words from a wise man's mouth are gracious, but a fool is consumed by his own lips*" (Ecclesiastes 10:12).

Jesus gave us this counsel: "*Out of the overflow of the heart the mouth speaks*" (Matthew 12:34b). You may wish to go to Him with a humble and repentant spirit, asking Him to place the love and presence of Christ in your heart. Your speech will reflect your heart.

Let's close these thoughts with these assuring words: "*Pleasant words are a honeycomb, sweet to the soul and healing to the bones*" (Proverbs 16:24).

God bless you as you use words to glorify God and encourage others!

Extra for Adults

From Isaiah 50:4-9 notice how listening and talking are related (verse 4). With carefully selected words and the Lord's help, how did this affect Isaiah's foes (verse 9)?

Consider Paul's admonition: "*Let your conversation be always full of grace, seasoned with salt, so that you may know how to answer everyone*" (Colossians 4:6). What would "*seasoned with salt*" mean to you?

Extra for Kids

1. When we sing songs and praise to God, can you guess to whom we also are singing and talking? (Look at Ephesians 5:19.)

2. When a bunch of people all talk at the same time, what do you hear? Can we be a good listener while we talk? Let's work on that.

As We Pray

1. Pray that God will help us not to talk too much.
2. Pray that God will give us the right words to pray and to use for others.
3. Pray for pastors, teachers, speakers, leaders and public speakers you know that God will give them wisdom in their words and a dependence on God in what they say.
4. Your own prayer(s):

11

When Going to Church Makes God Angry

"I want no more of your pious meetings."
— Isaiah 1:13 (*NLT*)

Does God ever ***not*** want us to go to church? Is there a time when He doesn't want us to sing spiritual songs, call on Him in prayer and place offerings in the offering plate? If our worship is similar to that of Judah in Isaiah's time of writing, the answer is, "Yes." Our worship would not be welcome. Consider the words of God through the prophet Isaiah. He expressed his displeasure of religious activity in Isaiah 1:1-20. As you read this passage, consider God's point of view.

The object of God's displeasure spoken in this passage occurred about 760 B.C. and reflected the emptiness of Judah's worship at the time. It wasn't that they weren't offering sacrifices, singing praises or praying. They were doing many outward acts of worship that were set forth by Moses years before, but the hearts of people in Judah were turned against God as they followed selfish and evil ways. Their sin led Isaiah to the point of comparing them to Sodom and Gomorrah and the judgment that came to those cities (verses 9, 10), and yet Judah continued going through the motions of worship. God even regarded their coming before Him with unrepentant hearts and sinful ways as a trampling of His courts.

What about our worship today? When we gather for worship, Bible study, prayer and other activities at church, is it possible these times are also without joy to God? Is our outward worship experience without a genuine heartfelt praise to Him? Do we have a serious neglect of love and support for the saints of the church?

The Apostle Paul warned Timothy of those who turned against God as they embraced selfish and sinful ways. Some were fraudulent leaders whose impact would hurt believers in the church (1 Timothy 6:20, 21).

I know a Navy veteran who, with a troubled heart and desire to share his needs, sought out a Christian chaplain aboard a U.S. Navy carrier. The chaplain announced early on, "What should we do? Play God?" Following the uttering of this bizarre statement, he had no depth or direction to offer the young seeker; and yet he was an authorized chaplain on a large U.S. ship. That sailor went away even more troubled and disillusioned. It seemed the message of the Christian faith could not help him.

Does God take pleasure in our worship of Him at church... in our daily walk with Christ? Are we practicing forms of church worship, but all the while like Judah have become sloppy and careless in our personal morals?

Once as a guest at a Bible camp, I joined the staff for a fun night. My heart sank when I saw the leaders and counselors watching a sensual and vulgar movie. No one moved to turn it off. One of my young heroes in life finally stepped in and changed it, much to the protest of the staff.

Do we need to have confession of sin to God as did Judah? Are we harboring sinful thoughts or hardness of heart toward God? The church or certain people? Read again the appeal to our hearts in Isaiah 1:18-20, noting the "*come,*" the "*obey*" and the "*promise*" of verse 18. Confess your sin; God forgives. Make your worship real! Avoid the phony witness of Judah as described in Isaiah 1.

Let's be part of the "light a candle, don't just curse the darkness" crowd! First, get right with God. Confess any sin to Him. Step out and approach people you may have had conflict with a heart of warmth and forgiveness. Notice the good news of Isaiah 1:18. Read it thoughtfully. Then enjoy worship as encouraged in 1 Chronicles 16:29: "*Ascribe to the LORD the glory due his name. Bring an offering and come before him; worship the LORD in the splendor of his holiness.*" Seek out worship partners who have a heart for God, the Bible and the message of hope in Christ! "*Come, let us bow down in worship, let us kneel before the LORD our Maker*" (Psalm 95:6). You will find God's presence and gladness in fellowship at church as never before.

Extra for Adults

Do you think our minds sometimes get so overwhelmed with busyness that we almost cannot focus on God during the worship service and our own Bible time? Is sin an issue? Or, is it a combination of both busyness and sin? Is it possible that we are simply not taught about worship?

My challenge to you is to write down some thoughts about how we can better worship Him in a way that pleases Him "*in spirit and in truth*" (John 4:24). Look up Hebrews 10:24, 25. Does the idea of our personal well being come into play when we read this passage?

Extra for Kids

Imagine that you are in church for a service. When I was a kid, I often thought about what I was going to do that afternoon, like riding my bike, playing sports and fishing. But we can do better than that. Can you think of things to pray about, some at church and some outside church to help you to worship better? Mark the boxes with your initials by each prayer you will consider *making your own prayer*.

Kid #1 **Kid #2** **Kid #3** **Kid #4**

"Lord, help the pastor to speak, and help me to listen."

☐ ☐ ☐ ☐

"Help me to see Your creation of the sky and the earth."

☐ ☐ ☐ ☐

"Help me to think of the words of the songs I sing."

☐ ☐ ☐ ☐

"Help me to forgive people and to love people around me as I love you."

☐ ☐ ☐ ☐

How about praying for your church leaders or your last year's Bible camp counselor? God knows kids need to get up after a service and move around, grab a treat and talk to friends. But when we are in a church meeting, we need to focus on the One who made us and loves us.

Would you be willing to interview your pastor or Sunday School teacher on worship? Ask them three questions:

1. How can I worship better at church?
2. How can I prepare for worship?
3. Do I worship all week long?

It would be interesting to see what they would say. Be sure to bring a notebook and pen, and ask God to help you.

As We Pray

1. Pray that we will acknowledge and confess any sin that may interfere with our worship.
2. Pray that we will not be drawn away by distractions when we worship Him.
3. Pray that we will have a rich time of worship both within the Christian family and in our everyday lives.
4. Pray that we will find both directness and gentleness in our encouraging others to worship Him in a way of His pleasing.
5. Your own prayer(s):

"Therefore, my dear brothers, stand firm. Let nothing move you. Always give yourselves fully to the work of the Lord, because you know that your labor in the Lord is not in vain." – 1 Corinthians 15:58

12

God, I Just Don't Need Your Help

"Ahaz said, 'I will not ask; I will not put the LORD to the test.'" **— Isaiah 7:12**

Ahaz, the King of Judah, consciously spurned God's help and cast rejection on the prophet Isaiah and his message. Isaiah 7:1-12 tells the story. The Lord offered deliverance in verses 3, 4 and 10, but Ahaz said, "No!"

What is the background of this story? Judah and King Ahaz were in trouble. Syrian forces were allied together with a rebellious Israel in their military campaign against Judah. Isaiah 7:2 (*NLT*) describes the tension:

> *The news had come to the royal court of Judah: "Syria is allied with Israel against us!" So the hearts of the king and his people trembled with fear, like trees shaking in a storm.*

God had said that the king and all of Judah could put their trust in Him and that their **enemies would not stand**. King Ahaz turned away from this promise.

Why would King Ahaz say no to God's help? Why would he even turn down God's offer to provide a sign (verses 11-12), putting a gracious God to a test for helping Judah? The key may partly be explained in verse 1. At an earlier point Jerusalem was able to throw back the attacks of the enemy. King Ahaz used his successes to place his reliance and confidence in himself and away from God.

If King Ahaz would have seen the coming destruction to his nation, himself and the subsequent kings, he might have thought differently! The king and his people eventually were to experience a total defeat by Assyrian armies.

There is a disappointing aspect in the refusal of King Ahaz to test and trust God. Ahaz had the advantage of having a father, Jotham, who as king did "*what was right in the eyes of the* LORD" (2 Chronicles 27:2); but early in his reign, Ahaz chose a different course. The sad story is told of his rebellion to God and the values of his father, Jotham. As a 20-year-old king Ahaz made idols to worship and even offered human sacrifice "*in the fire*" (2 Chronicles 28:3).

Have you ever been successful with your own solutions and efforts? Perhaps for a while you were able to deal with your problem successfully. However, we must realize that our lives on earth are complex, and we need God's help to face our challenges today and tomorrow. I encourage you to decide to lean on Him and place your trust in Him for this life and eternity.

Children, teens and adults, if you feel you have been drawn toward your own confidence instead of trusting God, won't you consider acknowledging your weakness and your need for the strength from your heavenly Father for the challenges of life?

Extra for Adults

Although this story has a sad outcome, you might be surprised what marvelous sign **does** come out of this passage. Here is a hint: "*The virgin will be with child and...*" (Isaiah 7:14). God uses even this faithless king to bring fantastic news. It is important for you to read Isaiah 7:13-16 for this sign.

The message to King Ahaz is a message for us as well: "*Unless your faith is firm, I cannot make you stand firm*" (Isaiah 7:9b *NLT*).

Extra for Kids

"No, I don't want your help!" That's what all of Mrs. Wilson's third grade class said to their teacher before the Christmas program one evening. A group of four kids was getting ready to go to the stage with their classmates to sing *We Three Kings* and to tell a story. Up they went in a line, holding high their large letters that spelled "STAR." One problem: they lined up backwards! Write the word "star" backwards:

_______ _______ _______ _______

It's good to try hard at what we do, and we will make mistakes. But it is important to let adults help sometimes. It is always good to ask God to help us love our brothers and sisters, to do well in school, to get over being sick, to do our chores. Ask for His help to forgive others, to be honest and to stop bad habits.

Look up Hebrews 13:5, 6 and fill in the blanks:

"'__________ will I leave you; __________ will I __________ you.' So we say with confidence, 'The __________ is my __________; I will not be __________.'"

As We Pray

1. "I need your help, Lord."
2. "Lord, help me to see Your desire to do great things for me and through me."
3. "Forgive us our sin of not always trusting in You. May we have faith in You when things go well and when things go poorly."
4. Your own prayer(s):

13

The Case of the Leaking Can

***"For my people have done two evil things: They have abandoned me—the fountain of living water. And they have dug for themselves cracked cisterns that can hold no water at all!"* — Jeremiah 2:13 (*NLT*)**

I got it cheap – like $5 at an auction in 1973. These six-gallon jerry cans like the one I bought are often carried in Jeeps and are tough and "cool" looking. I didn't have a Jeep, but I had a garage and have always been drawn to heavy-duty stuff. Upon getting home I examined my big rectangular gas can and noted that it was quite dirty and a little rusty inside. After using a tough cleaning solvent, water and giving the can a good shaking, I let it dry.

The next day I saw it still had some rust in the bottom, but somehow I believed in that can. I decided to continue to make the can right, so I asked a friend what he would do. He said to put a bunch of rocks in it and shake it vigorously for several minutes. So I did, then washed it with industrial-strength cleaner, rinsed it, drained it and let it dry. Then I cleaned it again.

A day later I looked at the now clean can and decided it was time to get some gas in it. At the station I began filling it and noticed after putting in one gallon of fuel that it was leaking pretty badly.

I had to do something quickly with the gas, so I tried pouring it into the car gas tank. The cans might be cool looking, but they sure pour badly without a funnel. Going home I reasoned that this was still a good gas can, but I needed to stop that leak.

Later that day I applied some guaranteed sealer. But when back at the gas station the next day, I discovered again that it still wouldn't hold gas.

Now my pride was kicking in. This was a good gas can, and I did get a good deal on it! Would the local welder help me and weld the leak shut? At the welding shop the busy welder said he would not be able to weld the leak, but he could put a new bottom on the whole jerry can.

For only $12 I got a new bottom welded to my jerry can, and finally I got a chance to fill it with several gallons of gas. Now satisfied that my total of $17 plus some spilt gas and my time, it was still a great deal for such a handsome gas can. After gassing it up, I went home and showed my dear wife. She nodded her head in partial understanding and loyal support. A moment later she queried, "What is that I smell?" I looked around the garage and finally at the jerry can. It was still leaking!

"Now there just must be a way to fix that can—***it's a good can!***"

Why do we try to use leaky gas cans or buckets that don't work? Sadly, Israel returned to use leaky cisterns with far more serious consequences than a leaky gas can.

Please read the fuller text in Jeremiah 2:10-13. The ***first*** of two evil things that the people of Israel did was to **walk away from their glorious God,** who was to them a fountain of life-giving water. The Psalmist had written that this God was their very "*fountain of life*" (Psalm 36:9 *KJV*), but Israel had abandoned their creator God, who had faithfully provided nothing less than protection, blessing, love and hope.

God said that the people committed a ***second*** evil by **creating a cistern from which all the water would drain out.** A cistern was a large, lined storage pit filled with water. The cistern assured that the water would be safe and then drawn out when needed for their physical needs. A leaky cistern was worthless!

Speaking for God, Jeremiah compared Israel's life choices to a leaky cistern. The people followed selfish, worldly and sinful behaviors to find happiness. The materials of choice for the building of the leaky cistern included money, power, pleasure, possessions and empty religious traditions. Other materials that went into its building were idol worship, corruption and sexual sins. Even the heavens were shocked by the trade off, and they "*shrink back in horror and dismay*" as Israel traded its fountain of living water for cracked cisterns (Jeremiah 2:13 *NLT*).

Have we built a faulty container in which to place some or all of our purpose, hopes and dreams? Have we abandoned the fountain of life, the One who created us and knows us best? Do our lives show us "drawing on" leaky cisterns? Could some of those be our obsession with jobs, hobbies, social standing, money or other things to satisfy our needs?

The issue is real for us today as we note Jesus' words,

Whosoever drinketh of this water shall thirst again: but whosoever drinketh of the water that I shall give him shall never thirst; but the water that I shall give him shall be in him a well of water springing up into everlasting life.
– John 4:13, 14 (*KJV*)

As you evaluate your life, are the precious things of God—worshipping Him, reading the Bible, serving and enjoying the church—at the top of your list, or do you stubbornly pour your life into leaky containers? This is an invitation to look at the Lordship of Christ in your life. We need to examine ourselves and perhaps repent before Him.

Pause a moment and think about where your heart and actions are today—the leaky cistern or the "fountain of life"? You may wish to confess your sin, ask for forgiveness and tell God you love Him before anything else.

Extra for Adults

The story of Demas is a rather sad one in the New Testament. He is mentioned twice in a good light: in Philemon 24 as a fellow worker and in Colossians 4:14 as one who sent greetings. However, Demas deserted the Apostle Paul at a crucial time toward the end of Paul's ministry. The reason given? The love of the "*things of this life.*" Read 2 Timothy 4:9-13. We don't know about Demas' ultimate standing with God, but we know the forces of the world drew him away from godly friends and the cause of the gospel. Think of the Apostle James' words: "*The friendship of the world is enmity with God*" (James 4:4 *KJV*). Let's always be on guard and keep Jesus Christ our first love!

Extra for Kids

Kids, help me think of children in the Bible who didn't have lives like a leaky bucket. They said "yes" to living for God. They said "no" to putting money, fun, toys, sports and stuff as being the most important things. (Those things aren't bad; they just can't come before the Lord.) Putting God behind first place is the "leaky bucket" way.

Let me help you get started in the "Good Bucket Kids' Club" with some of the following really cool kids in the Bible:

1. ___________ trusted his father (Genesis 22:7).
2. ______________, who would not sin like other youth (1Samuel 2:16-21, 26).
3. __________ __________ who helped a soldier to get well (2 Kings 5:2, 3).
4. Children were _________________ ________ ________ ______________ (Matthew 21:15).
5. Boy who gave his ______________ (John 6:9).
6. Joash was _____ years old when he became __________. He did what was ____ ____________________________ (2 Kings 11:21 and 12:1, 2).
7. Young boy who served D___________ and J_________________ obediently (1 Samuel 20:35-41).

You get something better than a blue ribbon for being in the "Good Bucket Kids' Club." Your dependence on God will bring you love, joy, peace, forgiveness, hope and heaven; and they won't leak out.

As We Pray

Pray slowly and thoughtfully:

> *Our Father which art in heaven, Hallowed be thy name. Thy kingdom come. Thy will be done in earth, as it is in heaven. Give us this day our daily bread. And forgive us our debts, as we forgive our debtors. And lead us not into temptation, but deliver us from evil: For Thine is the kingdom, and the power, and the glory, forever. Amen.*
>
> — Matthew 6:9-13 (*KJV*)

14

Fine Dining

"When your words came, I ate them; they were my joy and my heart's delight."

— Jeremiah 15:16

Eat God's Word? Why such a vivid metaphor? The early chapters of the book of Jeremiah record the story. Chosen from even before his conception in his mother's womb, God had planned for Jeremiah to speak to the people of Israel (1:9). The first chapter explains a coming judgment upon the people of Israel. They were called on to repent immediately, but God told Jeremiah they would resist.

The people became very angry with Jeremiah because of his proclamation of the bad times to come. As his ministry continued, this servant of God faced increasing bitterness and threatening opposition from the rebellious people. He cried out, "*I am hated everywhere I go ... they all curse me ... Please step in and help me*" (15:10, 15 *NLT*).

Time after time God did answer Jeremiah and provided words of comfort to this beleaguered prophet, and promises of divine physical protection were given to him. As time progressed, the stress seemed overwhelming to Jeremiah. God spoke assurance to him, "*Surely I will deliver you for a good purpose*" (verse 11).

One time when God comforted him during his troubles, Jeremiah proclaimed: "*When your words came,* **I ate them**; *they were my joy and my heart's delight, for I bear your name, O Lord God Almighty*" (verse 16). What a recovery!

About the same time God spoke to another prophet, Ezekiel, who recorded the effect of God's Word on his life: "*Then he said to me, 'Son of man, eat this scroll I am giving you and fill your stomach with it.' So* ***I ate it****, and it tasted as sweet as honey in my mouth*" (Ezekiel 3:3). Ezekiel chapters two and three describe God's provision as the Spirit lifted him up (Ezekiel 3:12, 14).

We need the food of God's Word! The apostle Peter said, "*As newborn babes, desire the sincere milk of the word, that ye may grow thereby*" (1 Peter 2:2 *KJV*).

Do you feast on God's Word, the Bible? God's Word provides us with His plan, promises and hope. Through it He counsels us daily. Like Jeremiah and Ezekiel, **you will be comforted by His Word** as you go through hard times. May God bless you as you grow each day, tasting His precious Word as the prophets of old did. It really is "fine dining"!

Extra for Adults

Check out these other passages that point to food for the soul:

1. Deuteronomy 8:3

2. Job 23:12

3. Psalm 119:103

Why do you think so many passages draw on food as a metaphor? Do you think it has anything to do with survival? See Matthew 4:4.

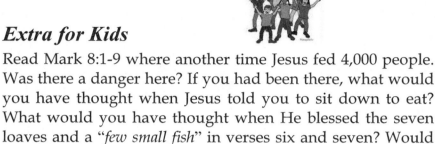

Extra for Kids

Read Mark 8:1-9 where another time Jesus fed 4,000 people. Was there a danger here? If you had been there, what would you have thought when Jesus told you to sit down to eat? What would you have thought when He blessed the seven loaves and a "*few small fish*" in verses six and seven? Would you have wondered how so many people like yourself would be fed? Kids, here is the important thing: they didn't go out into a desert area to get food. They went there to follow Jesus, who said, "*I am the bread of life. He who comes to me will never go hungry*" (John 6:35). That means that if you follow Jesus, He will be your Guide, Helper and Savior!

As We Pray

1. Thank God for our daily food.

2. Thank God for being our provider.

3. Pray we will see the importance of God's Word to feed our hearts and that we read it and love the author!

4. Your own prayer(s):

EXTRA, EXTRA

Can you connect the passage with the reference?

"Man does not live on bread alone but on every word that comes from the mouth of the Lord."	Job 23:12
"Like newborn babies, crave pure spiritual milk, so that by it you may grow up in your salvation."	Deuteronomy 8:3
"How sweet are your words to my taste, sweeter than honey to my mouth!"	Jeremiah 15:16
"When your words came, I ate them; they were my joy and my heart's delight."	1 Peter 2:2
"I have treasured the words of His mouth more than my daily bread."	Psalm 119:11
"I have hidden your word in my heart that I might not sin against you."	Psalm 119:103

15

Stuck in the Mud

"So the officials took Jeremiah from his cell and lowered him by ropes into an empty cistern in the prison yard ... There was no water in the cistern, but there was a thick layer of mud at the bottom, and Jeremiah sank down into it."

— Jeremiah 38:6 (*NLT*)

"We don't like what the prophet of God said so we dropped him into a deep, muddy well." That could have been the report to King Zedekiah from the officials listed in Jeremiah 38:1.

I don't like mud, and I just can't see why I would ever go into it "on purpose." I cannot identify with the idea of mud runs, mud motocross or mud wrestling! My unhappy experience with mud as a kid might be part of the reason.

It started out as a great warm day in May. Bursting with energy, my friend Chucky and I started out on our six-mile bike ride to Medicine Lake. Our bikes were loaded up with poles, fishing gear, lunch, buckets, knives and a spare jacket. It was special because I was trying out my brand new bike. Half way there we decided to stop for water at an elderly couple's farm. A problem came when I decided not to go around a very big garden located between us and the house.

My youthful calculation failed to note that the garden, being unplanted, was not just a little wet. I charged forward, riding my bike with all my gear. I became nearly frantic as I just got in deeper and deeper in the mud. Finally, getting off my bike and now walking in deep mud, I began pushing my ill-fated bicycle forward. Before long my bike became stuck deep into the mud. The sticky soil covered my shoes by several inches. I abandoned my bike and my fishing equipment in the mud, and barely made it to the grassy area. I was horrified when I looked back at my bike. It must have looked funny to our elderly friends watching from their window: my bike was buried in a foot of mud, sticking straight up—ditto for the fishing pole a few feet away.

I felt it was about the worst thing that had happened to me in my 11 years of life. I was in deep trouble! How would I explain this loss to my parents? I trudged up to the house, knocked on the door and explained my awful problem.

The man came out, and without a word carried some planks from the barn. Starting at the grassy area, he laid the boards across the mud to my bike. I thought he was as strong as a horse as he raised my mud-caked bike out and then carried it to safety. Relief and joy replaced my misery.

Please read the fuller text in Jeremiah 38:1-13, which details events after leaders complained about Jeremiah. Jeremiah had an experience with mud, and it was much more serious than mine. After sinking down into the mud and being without food for days, Jeremiah was in danger of losing his life!

Why did angry men treat an honorable prophet so cruelly? The message Jeremiah brought was stern and called for repentance. On top of this, he proclaimed certain judgment for Judah's people and nation because of their evil way of living. God would use the empire of Babylon to conquer Judah and destroy Jerusalem, according to Jeremiah.

This great prophet was faithful to God but was met with ridicule and cruelty from the people. Speaking of prophets and people of faith like Jeremiah, the writer of Hebrews declared, "*The world was not worthy of them*" (Hebrews 11:38). Although harshly imprisoned and confined in a muddy well, God still had His watchful eye and caring hands on Jeremiah, who was eventually rescued.

As believers in Jesus Christ, we're following what God has called on us to do when we share the gospel of hope with neighbors and friends. We're obedient when we teach the principles of the Bible in a loving way.

The Bible warns us of the consequences of a godless life and points us to a life of redemption and hope. Sometimes, like Jeremiah's message, ours is a serious warning for the need of each person to repent of sin and to receive Jesus by faith as our Savior. Like Jeremiah, we, too, will face opposition. In fact, Jesus warned us in the gospel of John 15:18-21 that we would be hated.

I don't know what kind of mud you may have gotten yourself into as you have sincerely set out to serve the Lord, but note the renewed promises first given in Genesis 28:15 and then repeated in Hebrews 13:5b: "*God has said, 'Never will I leave you, never will I forsake you.'*" If you get stuck in the mud, honor Him by calling to Him for help.

The book of Hebrews also teaches us the importance of encouragement from fellow believers: "*Encourage one another daily*" (3:13). While help from immediate family is really important, I strongly urge you to have a small support group to lean on. Other believers are an important source of help when we get stuck in the mud. If there is no small support group available to you, God may lead you to start one.

Extra for Adults

King Zedekiah did not take Jeremiah's warnings to heart. Read Jeremiah 52:1-30 for an end look at the king, Jeremiah and the nation of Judah. Then read Jeremiah 1:13, 14. Notice how completely God's words were fulfilled.

Extra for Kids

1. What are some of your experiences with mud?
2. Has anyone in your household been stuck in the mud?
3. What do you think Jeremiah hated the most: the mud, the darkness, no food and water or his loneliness?
4. Can you trust God even when you are in a tough spot?

As We Pray

1. Thank Him for the day, light, dryness, food and friends.
2. Thank God for the reliability of His Word and also that we can know God cares for His own.
3. Pray that God will help us when we are hurt by others or when we are stuck in the mud to rely on Him for our safety.
4. Pray that we would be willing as God leads to go to a small group of believing friends to regularly pray with and be encouraged.
5. Your own prayer(s):

16

Don't Be Happy When Your Brother or Sister Gets Hurt!

"You should not look down on your brother in the day of his misfortune."

— Obadiah 12

Obadiah is the shortest book in the Old Testament. Read verses 1-16.

As brothers, Jacob and Esau were able to patch up many of the problems they experienced over the years. But their descendants were in conflict until both Jacob's nation Judah and Esau's nation Edom each met calamity.

When fierce invaders from Babylon overwhelmed Judah, the response of the people of Edom was to rejoice in Judah's misery (verse 12). While the Edomites were blood relatives, this did not keep them from plundering the land of Judah and even killing those trying to escape the ravages of Babylon (verse 14). The prophet Obadiah brought to the Edomites and surviving Jews the message that God would bring judgment upon Edom for hurting Judah, their brother (verse ten).

Smugly regarding themselves as secure, the citizens of Edom celebrated to witness Judah destroyed and even participated in their destruction. The Edomites believed themselves untouchable by any nation. They thought of themselves as a tough people living in a mountainous region that could not be penetrated. But God said in verses three and four,

> *The pride of your heart has deceived you, you who live in the clefts of the rocks and make your home on the heights, you who say to yourself, "Who can bring me down to the ground?" Though you soar like the eagle and make your nest among the stars, from there I will bring you down, declares the* L*ORD*.

The judgment from God came in 164 B.C. by the Maccabees, who were fierce Judean loyalists determined to rid their homeland of idol worship and those who practiced it. The Edomites, whom they conquered, lost their idols and their nation. The destruction was complete. The kingdom of Edom was prophesied to "*be destroyed forever*" (verse ten). It is remarkable that the Edomites as a separate people disappeared completely from history by the time the Greeks were in power under Alexander the Great.

Noting with surprise the extinction of the Edomites, one encyclopedia described it as a mystery that such a complete destruction of Edom's people and kingdom took place. It is not a mystery to those who believe the prophet Obadiah. The Bible tells us clearly: it was God's judgment upon a people who had severely abused Judah.

What else does the book of Obadiah tell us? In plain words, **God does pay attention to how we treat other people**! Psalm 103:6 says, "*The* L*ORD works righteousness and justice for* *all the oppressed.*" Solomon reflected on a day we will all give account for our treatment of those around us: "*God will bring to judgment both the righteous and the wicked, for there will be a time for every activity, a time for every deed*" (Ecclesiastes 3:17). Do we want to please God? Hebrews 13:16 tells us to "*do good*" and "*to share.*" Sounds simple but hard to do sometimes, right? Let's do good and share because we love God. It would be easy to say that this is a nice thought and then to leave the thought on the page. Would you now decide to become more aware of people in need around you and to ask God for ways to show goodness to them?

Extra for Adults

It is interesting to note how even a defeated nation like Edom could still have an evil influence upon Judah. After the Edomites were defeated, King Amaziah brought Edom's idolatry home. The king and nation knew *only the Lord God was to be worshipped.* The result brought about great losses for Judah. Observe the serious consequences of the people and nation and what the king did with the items he brought back from Edom. The Edomites left a dismal legacy.

We, too, have to be careful to resist evil and idolatry. The Apostle Paul said to the church at Rome: "*Don't let evil conquer you, but conquer evil by doing good*" (Romans 12:21 *NLT*).

Extra for Kids

1. Sometimes we see our brothers and sisters in trouble. I hope you don't laugh at them.

2. God wants you to help them when they are in need. Can you think of a time your brother, sister or friend was hurting; and you were able to help them? (You know how

nice it is for you when you get hurt and someone comes to help and comfort you.)

3. Think of three ways you sometimes need help, and write them here:
   a. ______________________________
   b. ______________________________
   c. ______________________________

Next time you see someone needing help like you listed, won't you be good and help them?

As We Pray

1. We are to "*be kind to one another, tenderhearted*" to one another (Ephesians 4:32 *KJV*). Let's pray that God will help us to not be rude or indifferent to others and their needs, even if they are indifferent to us.
2. Think of someone who has been struggling with illness, financial problems, family problems or some personal problem. Pray for them. Then tomorrow consider phoning them just to tell them you were thinking of them or send them a friendship card. You will be blessed yourself!
3. Your own prayer(s):

17

Lord, Please Put My Bully in a Cage

"Love your enemies!" — Matthew 5:44

Well, that's different! Love? Isn't it just a natural reaction to despise, even hate those who would oppose us or do us harm? A fuller text is Matthew 5:43-44: "*You have heard that it was said, 'Love your neighbor and hate your enemy.' But I tell you: Love your enemies and pray for those who persecute you.*"

Years ago I was familiar with a situation where the manager of a well-known large firm humiliated unsuspecting employees, and caused many to leave because of unresolved issues. This manager would stand at a work station until the troubled employee emptied the desk and shelves of all personal items. Usually no kind words were expressed on the part of the manager during the unhappy departure of the employee. The final words from his mouth were often, "Don't ask for a reference." Then he would call security personnel to escort the employee off the property. Unfortunately, there were more than just a few workers who left his supervision and experienced hurtful effects.

If an enemy is defined as one who is hostile to another person, it seems as though this manager had been an enemy to several people. Jesus said, "*Love your enemies,*" a response that is counter to human nature when we are intentionally hurt by someone. Our western media often looks for radical stories to attract listeners and viewers. In the same way a follower of Jesus can be radical, attracting many outside the faith just by loving his enemies!

The person I hated the most in my life was a neighborhood bully I knew when I was only ten years old. He was 13 and very large. He would grab me or my bike and threaten me. I thought he was a monster, and I feared him greatly. I was scared to go out. I absolutely regarded him as an enemy. I didn't know Tae Kwon Do, only Tae Kwon Run! But then he'd grab my bike.

I wonder what I would have thought if someone had told me to love and pray for my bully. That would have been a revolutionary thought for me as a child! I might have plugged into that thought if some believer had sat down with me and shared how Jesus wanted me to love my enemy, and "*do good, and lend, expecting nothing in return; and your reward will be great*" (Luke 6:35a *NASB*).

In a sense we are all children, and we are learning. When we are hurt by someone, we need to remember that Jesus taught us to **love our enemies and pray for them.**

Let's look at this from the opposite point of view. Are you a bully? Most of us would say no, but think about this a moment. Couldn't anyone who uses control over another for personal gain or simply a sense of power without regard for other's feelings or needs be a bully? Let's examine our own hearts.

If you are a manipulating person who abuses people—or a flat out bully—consider these words warning of God's wrath: "*For those who are self-seeking and who reject the truth and follow evil, there will be wrath and anger*" (Romans 2:8). If you are a follower of Christ, consider these words: "*Be kind to each other, tenderhearted*" (Ephesians 4:32 NLT).

Extra for Adults

Read Matthew 5:43-48. What do the believers have in common with nonbelievers in this passage (verse 45)? How do verses 46 and 47 relate to what Jesus said in verse 44? Let's follow the Savior and love others who despitefully use us at school, at work and in our neighborhood. Isn't it interesting how Jesus connected loving and praying for enemies with "*sons of your Father in heaven*" (verses 44-45)?

Extra for Kids

1. Is there someone who bullies you, or someone who seems to want to hurt you in some way? Someone who calls you names? Embarrasses you? That is tough to deal with. Ask God to give you love for that person and begin to pray for him or her.

2. Talk to a parent or a friend who loves Jesus. Ask that person to pray for you, to encourage you to love and pray for people who are bullies or hard to get along with.

As We Pray

1. Ask God to help us love in a way that is not natural for us, to see big-time needs in our enemies and to pray for them.

2. Pray we won't be discouraged as we fall short of loving our enemies.

3. Pray that we would strengthen our friendships with our brothers and sisters in Christ. Pray that God would draw us closer to these fellow believers and that we would be built up by them to help us face personal opposition.

4. Pray for enemies to become friends and followers of Jesus.

5. Your own prayer(s):

18

No, Jesus, You Have It Wrong

"Peter took him* [Jesus] *aside and began to rebuke him, 'Never, Lord!' he said. 'This shall never happen to you!'"

— Matthew 16:22

Read Matthew 16:21-23, the passage where Jesus spoke of His own death and resurrection.

Why would Peter say this? Wouldn't he know how to regard and to speak with Jesus, of whom he said was "*the Christ, the Son of the living God*" (Matthew 16:16)? It is rather easy to look down upon Peter's life and character, as some seem to do. I regard him as a hero, but at this moment Peter was struggling. I believe there are four principle reasons why Peter rebuked Jesus.

The ***first*** was **his passion and love for Christ**. It was to Jesus he cried out to save him from sinking in the rough seas. Jesus took him by the hand and led him to the ship (Matthew 14:29-31). Peter loved the Master but had his own ideas of how it should go for a God and Savior. That did not include torture from the religious leaders that would lead to death.

The ***second*** reason is that **the idea of Jesus being the king of Israel on earth** was not far from the minds of many Jewish believers, including the disciples. After the feeding of the 5,000 and with Peter nearby, the people "*intended to come and make him* [Jesus] *king by force*" (John 6:15). Then just before Jesus ascended into heaven, the disciples asked, "*Lord, are you at this time going to restore the kingdom to Israel?*" (Acts 1:6).

It is fair to say the earthly and political kingdom was frequently on Peter's mind. At the moment when Jesus explained His coming death, Peter thought that would be disastrous. Having Jesus as Messiah/King over the throne of Israel? That was a dream come true. Jesus was the best hope for Israel! That Jesus would suffer and die? That we would lose this political momentum? Never! Yet as the Apostle Paul wrote in Romans 5:8-10 (*NLT*) "*God showed his great love for us by sending Christ to die.*" The passage goes on to say that our "*friendship with God was restored.*" Jesus' mission was more than being the King of Israel.

Δ

The ***third*** reason Peter rebuked Jesus was because as far as Peter was concerned, being a disciple of Jesus was **a spiritual calling with the master teacher/healer**. While traveling with this divine champion for over two years, Peter had seen many signs and miracles from Christ. Now he and the disciples were given "*authority to drive out evil spirits and to heal every disease and sickness*" (Matthew 10:1). Peter knew there was a greater cause for which he was called. He was called for the kingdom of heaven by the Christ.

Peter also liked that Jesus dealt with hypocrisy and insincerity from anyone, including pompous religious people. Peter had witnessed the Master's dealing with the hardest questions about the law, faith, love, morality and hope for the future. This Jesus was the Son of God, who filled empty hearts with His blessed divine presence. As far as Peter was concerned, this Savior and movement were not going to be interrupted by those who had been shown to be selfish, critical and sometimes immoral. Besides, the opposition had been shown to be weak when confronted with the Master. With all that we have going for us, Peter would have reasoned, why would we go through the indignity of the suffering and death of our Savior? Lose all heavenly momentum we have going? Never!

That leads to the ***fourth*** and most significant reason Peter had taken the bold step of rebuking Jesus. **He simply did not understand**. After the resurrection Jesus described the two Emmaus-bound disciples as "*foolish*" and "*slow of heart to believe*" (Luke 24:25). Jesus "*opened their minds so that they could understand*" that the Old Testament had said that "*the Christ will suffer and rise from the dead*" (Luke 24:45, 46).

Because he did not understand why the Christ would die on the cross, Peter made the extraordinarily bold move of taking Jesus aside and with passion and rebuke told him, "*Never, Lord. This shall never happen!*" (Matthew 16:22). But it was God's plan that it would happen.

Read the following Bible passages. Notice how the Apostle Peter years later came to have a new understanding as recorded in the third Scripture passage:

> *But he was pierced for our transgressions, he was crushed for our iniquities; the punishment that brought us peace was upon him, and by his wounds we are healed. We all, like sheep, have gone astray, each of us has turned to his own*

way; and the L*ORD has laid on him the iniquity of us all.*
— Isaiah 53:5, 6 ♦ Words of ***Isaiah***

I am the good shepherd. The good shepherd lays down his life for the sheep. — John 10:11 ♦ Words of ***Jesus***

For you know that it was not with perishable things such as silver or gold that you were redeemed from the empty way of life handed down to you from your forefathers, but with the precious blood of Christ, a lamb without blemish or defect.
— 1 Peter 1:18, 19 ♦Words of Apostle ***Peter***

Peter had learned that Jesus had it right. This indescribable gift was God's plan.

Yet to all who received him, to those who believed in his name, he gave the right to become children of God.
— John 1:12 ♦ Words of Apostle ***John***

Is Jesus, who gave His life, your Savior?

____

♦ ***Your words***

If you feel His Spirit speaking to your heart and want to receive Him, please go to the "Steps to Peace with God" at the back of this book for help.

Extra for Adults

Some time before Jesus and the disciples went to Gethsemane where Jesus was betrayed, the disciples were told that they would abandon Him (Matthew 26:31). Jesus actually was drawing attention to the prophecy of Zechariah 13:7. Over 500 years earlier the prophet spoke of events around Jesus' crucifixion and also about the history of Israel. Read Zechariah 13:7-9. Notice that God will refine Israel through hardships, and a remnant will believe. Note the detail of the description of Jesus in Zechariah 9:9-10! Praise God for His thoughtful foreknowledge!

Extra for Kids

Hey, kids, I've got a question for you. Imagine you are over 18 years old and put in jail for breaking the law for stealing a lawn mower or for getting gas at the filling station and not paying for it. Do you think it is understandable that you should be punished?

Once a law was broken by a man named Chuck Colson. He was in prison for months, and his family was suffering because he was not home to help them. A former governor of Minnesota, Al Quie, **offered to go to jail** for Chuck Colson so Chuck could be with his hurting family. Mr. Quie would have gone to jail in place of his friend. If you were in jail and were given freedom by someone taking your place, how would you feel? Happy, I think. Jesus did take your place for your sins. This is very happy news!

As We Pray

1. Thank God for the great price Jesus paid at the cross for your sins and the sins of the world through our indescribable gift.

2. Pray for friends and loved ones who don't know Christ.

3. Pray that God's Spirit would go before us to touch the hearts of those who need Him as we tenderly, yet directly, share the good news of Jesus.

4. Your own prayer(s):

19

When 7 Is Not the Perfect Number

"I'm going to up it to seven times!"

***"Then Peter came to him and asked, 'Lord, how often should I forgive someone who sins against me? Seven times?' 'No, not seven times,' Jesus replied, 'but seventy times seven.'"* — Matthew 18:21, 22 (*NLT*)**

Peter was struck with the idea of reconciliation with brothers in the faith, which Jesus had been teaching the disciples as recorded in verses 15-20. As Peter thought about this, he wanted to apply it in such a way that he would exceed even the standards of the Jewish rabbis, who had fixed a "high" limit of "three" forgivenesses. Peter's question of verse 21 assumed that more forgiveness is better, but that there was to be a limit in forgiving fellow believers. One writer offered a good description of Peter's mindset:

> The Jews were very fond of defining and limiting moral obligations, as if they could be accurately prescribed by number. Christ demolishes this attempt to define by law the measure of grace.[3]

As Peter approached Jesus, he was quite confident he was proposing a very generous standard for forgiving someone. He proposed the generous number of "*seven times,*" which meant somehow that on the eighth offense, one could shut the door on forgiving that person anymore!

Jesus gave a response (one could say a "sizzling" response) that surprised Peter, but continued to introduce him to the spirit of grace that would be soon reflected in the Christian gospel: "*No, not seven times ... but seventy times seven!*" (18:22). In other words, there is no limit, Peter, in the number of times for you to forgive others!

Read the parable in Matthew 18:23-35 that the Lord gave Peter following Peter's **seven times proposal**. It's an interesting story about a compassionate king and an unmerciful servant. Reflect on how it related to Peter's understanding of God's standards for forgiveness and grace.

Rich lessons for Peter and for us come out of this parable. The debt-ridden servant pleaded, even falling down begging, for patience from the king to give him time to pay the debt. The king was "*filled with pity for him*" (18:27). As a result, the debt was forgiven. The servant then benefited greatly by keeping his wife, children and all he owned. That part brings us warm feelings, doesn't it? (Peter probably didn't see himself as this servant at this point in the parable, but he would later.)

Jesus continued the parable, explaining that the forgiven servant left the king and went to a fellow servant who owed the first servant a much smaller amount yet had the fellow servant arrested and thrown in jail! That seems just plain cruel!

The parallel to Peter could not have been missed. Jesus Christ, the King, forgave Peter's many offenses, resulting in many blessings for him. Peter essentially asked Jesus in verse 21 if there couldn't be a limit to forgiveness toward others who were fellow believers and brothers and sisters in the faith (18:15, 35). As Peter contemplated his own forgiven sins, he now would have felt the sting of his hypocrisy. Jesus made it clear that He was talking to Peter.

God forgave all Peter's offenses, which like ours today, were many! If we have made Him our Savior, **He has forgiven all of our offenses**. We must not limit our forgiveness toward others!

Δ

Our Savior added a touch of beauty with His last nine words about forgiveness in verse 35 (*NLT*). He said, "*That's what my heavenly Father will do to you if you refuse* ***to forgive your brothers and sisters from your heart.***" Peter was not to count, nor should we calculate 70 times seven. ***Forgive from your heart,*** which is to have the love of God work through you; and don't calculate incoming offenses.

Several years ago I was in a training seminar with missionaries from the fine organization of SIM (Serving in Mission). Upon completion of a certain session, I felt I needed to seek out a certain lady because of an unintended dispute we had gotten mired in during a discussion period. As I was looking for her, she came up behind me, said she was sorry and gave me a hug saying, "I like to keep short accounts." I apologized to this missionary for my part in the exchange and later thought her perspective on conflict was right. All believers should keep short accounts! Let's be quick to forgive!

I love Ephesians 4:32 (*NLT*), "*Be kind to each other, tenderhearted, forgiving one another, just as God through Christ has forgiven you*." Let each of us look at our own hearts. Have you been a forgiving person?

Extra for Adults

What can we do when we have experienced a broken relationship with a Christian brother or sister, who just does not want restoration of fellowship and love? Unhappily, it sometimes happens that genuine expressions for reconciliation are met with coldness, and efforts to talk are met with accusations. Possibly gossip or slander has been directed against you. Sometimes unresponsive people excuse the need to deal with a problem by saying the offense upon them was so great they cannot talk about it. Sadly, they might not want the relationship resolved. They might even say, "The offense was too great!" The unresponsive brother or sister may look upon themselves as not having much need to be forgiven because "they" have walked the "straight and narrow." Despite the Scriptures' high regard for godly counsel, the resisting person in their pride may not want counsel, wanting to avoid subjects which would reflect badly on them or expose their prideful heart.

Let me offer some suggestions:

1. If you haven't already, **examine yourself** to see if you have any of the attitudes mentioned in the previous paragraph. "*If we say we have no sin, we deceive ourselves*" (1 John 1:8 *KJV*). Confess your sin to God. Ask forgiveness from any person involved for "your part" in the conflict.

2. While you experience this hurt, **let God comfort you**. "*Let the peace that comes from Christ rule in your hearts*" (Colossians 3:15 *NLT*).

3. **Stay soft**. Don't lose the special touch of God in your heart just because someone hurts you. "*Clothe yourselves with tenderhearted mercy, kindness, humility, gentleness and patience*" (Colossians 3:12 *NLT*).
4. **Pray for the person** in conflict. "*Pray for each other*" (James 5:16).
5. **Let it go**. "*Give all your worries and cares to God, for He cares about you*" (1 Peter 5:7 *NLT*).
6. **Move on** with other special relationships. "*But if we walk in the light, as he is in the light, we have fellowship one with another*" (1 John 1:7 *KJV*).
7. **Continue to be in the Word** and grow. "*As newborn babes, desire the sincere milk of the word, that ye may grow thereby*" (1 Peter 2:2 *KJV*).

Extra for Kids

For today's "extra" on forgiveness, I've asked my wife to tell a story about her life:

Hi kids! My name is Grandma Jean, and I'm grandma to nine special grandkids. I'd like to tell you what happened to me when I was a little girl and what I learned about forgiveness.

My mom and dad divorced when I was six years old. Later my parents each married someone else. Then I had a sister and a brother plus another sister and two brothers. Unfortunately, my parents' second marriages ended in divorce, too. I was the only child my dad had, but I lived with my mom, sister and brother. Because of all the changes I moved a lot (12 locations in four cities), so I attended 13 schools in 12 years.

Even though Dad lived only a few miles away, I had little contact with him. A few times he took me to the lake to go fishing. On some Sunday mornings he'd pick me up after church, take me to his new house, and then bring me back to church for youth group that evening. Even though we were together at times, my relationship with my dad was pretty much an empty one. When Dad and I were together, he didn't do much with me personally, and we didn't have any dad and daughter talks. I couldn't get close to Dad.

What I remember is being hurt because Dad never came to any of my programs or concerts. Every February when the Camp Fire Girls Sweetheart Banquet for dads and daughters was held, I had to sit alone. It would have been fun to play my violin for Dad at my orchestra concerts in my 3rd*–*12th *grades, or to have my dad attend my Christmas programs at school and church. Dad was missing at my confirmation, too. In high school I couldn't get a driver's license because my dad didn't want me driving his car, and Mom couldn't afford one. He did come to my high school graduation and wedding, but Dad missed most of my life.*

As a married adult my dad missed a lot of time not only with me, but also with my wonderful husband and three fun boys. While not living far from us, Dad came to see us only three times in 25 years! It would have been so nice to see my dad anywhere of his choosing; but when he came, it was because he was coaxed.

In the middle of this, my stepfather abused me.

I had lots of reasons to be bitter with God and family; but God used my church family – especially my pastors and their wives – to love me, help me and tell me so many Bible stories. My church family and Bible camp workers taught me about Jesus and how to live for Him. One day I wasn't sure I really had invited Jesus into my heart and be my Savior, so I lay on my mom's bed and talked to the Lord. Then I knew Jesus was mine!

Because of my difficult life as a child and being hurt over and over, I could have become angry – or even worse, bitter and resentful. God had a plan for me, though, and helped me to forgive Dad as well as love, care and pray for him. In fact, God allowed me to lead Dad to invite Jesus into his life ten months before he died!

So kids, if someone has hurt you and they ask you to forgive them, you need to forgive them. Remember that God **always** *forgives us when we ask. Even though someone close to you has been mean or neglectful and you are still hurting, ask God to give you an understanding and tender heart. Even if they don't say "I'm Sorry,"* **love** *them anyway, and especially pray for them.*

As We Pray

1. "Thank you, dear Lord and King of our lives, for forgiving us."

2. "Lord, help us to be forgiving in our hearts and find ways to communicate this to others."

3. "Help us to love the unloving people we meet and those we must be with regularly who are hard to deal with. Give us the words to say."

4. "Help us to develop deeper friendships in Christ that we can help one another."

5. Your own prayer(s):

[3] A. Lukyn Williams. *The Pulpit Commentary on Matthew, Vol. 15*. Grand Rapids: Eerdmans (1978), 213.

"He will wipe away every tear from their eyes. There will be no more death or mourning or crying or pain, for the old order of things has passed away."

– Revelation 21:4

20

Please Remove Those Pesky Kids!

(Part 1)

***"People were bringing little children to Jesus to have him touch them, but the disciples rebuked them. When Jesus saw this, he was indignant. He said to them, 'Let the little children come to me, and do not hinder them, for the kingdom of God belongs to such as these.'"* — Mark 10:13, 14**

Read the entire passage recorded in Mark 10:13-16. Imagine this scene: Jesus had been teaching on some very heavy issues including sin and marriage. As people began to bring children to have Jesus "*touch them,*" the disciples tried to remove this distraction, to "correct" this problem by rebuking the parents and children who would bother the Teacher. Jesus promptly showed indignation (verse 14) and said they should allow the children to come to Him!

Let's face it—sometimes kids are annoying; perhaps kids are often annoying. Our children and grandchildren have been a blessing to our hearts, but they were also attention-craving and action-packed little people. Nor do I think the children who came to Jesus were very compliant, almost dazed or angelic little beings sitting on His lap as depicted in countless classical and modern art images. I think they were normal little people looking for special attention. Parents urging their children toward Jesus were also part of the picture.

The children who came to Jesus were most likely squirmy, competitive little bundles with ever-moving arms and legs. Some were probably clean, others may have had dirty hair or food stains on their faces. One might have brought a pet lizard to show Jesus. Their little fingers could have found Jesus' nose and ears.

With Jesus' reputation for healing, I imagine them solemnly showing Jesus their "owies." After all, that's what the big people did! This scene made the disciples very uncomfortable; but for both parents and kids it was an opportunity to be close to the One whom they had heard great things about, the One with a divine touch. While Jesus certainly could make them compliant and docile, I believe He took them as they were. That is an important part of the message of this passage to us.

In a way the children seeking to be with Jesus and wanting to be touched by Him are like all of us. We, too, come to Him with all our blemishes and imperfections. We want attention, and we want to be with people whom we feel can help us. Adults might not call them "owies," but we have hurts physically, emotionally and spiritually that draw us to Christ.

The good news for children and adults is that Jesus **wants** us to come to Him. He made that clear early in His ministry. In the synagogue in Nazareth, He was given a scroll of the prophet Isaiah to read. He read from Isaiah 61:1-2, where the passage says the Lord sent Jesus to preach the good news and to release the oppressed. As eyes were fastened on Jesus, He said, "*Today this scripture is fulfilled in your hearing*" (Luke 4:21). Listeners that day got the message: Jesus was the very One God sent. You may read this moving passage in its entirety in Luke 4:16-22.

We need to go to Him every day to get help for our "owies," to find release from our burdens and to hear the good news!

Extra for Adults and Kids

I'm not really sure why some adults brought me to a Santa Claus in a mall one time when I was a little kid. At home I was taught there was no Santa Claus, but there was Jesus. That seemed OK to me; but when I was on Santa's lap, it was kind of an awkward moment. Below is a line from a carol often sung during the Christmas season. Help me fill in the blanks below by using the name Santa or Jesus.

> ___________ knows when you are sleeping ___________ knows when you're awake. ___________ knows if you've been good or bad, so be good for goodness sake!

I hope you are putting the name **Jesus** in the blanks, because He is for real! "*And he took the children in his arms, put his hands on them and blessed them*" (Mark 10:16). Jesus has the best lap! Jesus is touching your heart right now if you believe in Him.

Extra for Kids

Think on these verses as you fill in the blanks with the words on the right column:

Matthew 11:28 – "*Come to me, all you who are __________ and burdened, and I will give you __________.*"

Psalm 51:2 – "*Wash away all my __________ and __________ me from my sin.*"

1 Corinthians 6:11 – "*And this is what some of you were. But you were __________, you were sanctified, you were __________ in the name of the Lord Jesus Christ and by the Spirit of our God.*"

Psalm 51:7 – "*Cleanse me with hyssop, and I will be __________; wash me, and I will be __________ than snow.*"

whiter
justified
clean
weary
iniquity
washed
rest
cleanse

As We Pray

1. Pray to see with clarity Jesus' testimony from Luke 4:21.
2. Pray that our hearts would be warmed because our Savior calls us to come to Him for comfort, healing and release from oppression.
3. Pray that we will place ourselves in His care and trust Him whether we go through good times or bad.
4. Pray for God to give us the words of comfort to share with the sick, the hurting and the restless who may be near us.
5. Your own prayer(s):

21

Please Remove Those Pesky Kids!

(Part 2)

***"And he said: 'I tell you the truth, unless you change and become like little children, you will never enter the kingdom of heaven. Therefore, whoever humbles himself like this child is the greatest in the kingdom of heaven.'"* — Matthew 18:3, 4**

In Part 1, we saw how the Lord Jesus became indignant when the disciples rebuked the people who were bringing children to Him. The welcome of the children was clear as the Savior took them in His arms and blessed them. The high value of little children was a big teaching moment for the disciples, and still is for us today. As recorded by Matthew, the next lesson the disciples were to learn about children was that these little ones were examples of faith.

Jesus was surrounded by the chosen disciples, who would carry on His work. They also had some authority and exercised it. The way they saw it, little people were about to mess up the work that the big people felt was important. After all, when it came to protocol, especially around Jesus, they knew best—at least they thought so. Adults knew how to cook, manage a house and even tend to a physical wound; they oversaw education and businesses. The disciples felt that one reason they were there was to control the situation, and in this case it was the children.

With an audience of grownups, Jesus pointed out the example of these little people in respect to their faith. **This** was a reversal. The norm back then—and today—is to think and act like adults, but Jesus said to think and act like children!

That must have been quite a teaching moment for the disciples, just like today when a child figures out a troubling computer problem. Children, you have it right. We are amazed: "My computer now works!" Jesus was saying the children have it right; they have the right kind of faith!

Jesus **wanted** the children to come to Him. Their place in God's kingdom on earth and in heaven was real. The children were bona fide members of God's kingdom and provided an example of faith for the disciples to follow. Jesus demonstrated that children were to be highly regarded. Do we regard children as highly as we should?

In a way that pleased God, these little ones put their faith and trust in Jesus. The children were not thinking about ambitious goals, worldly competitions or the religious issues of grownups. Rather, their model of faith was turning away from self and toward a simple but real trust in Christ. Without that kind of faith by young and old, we will not enter His kingdom—Jesus said that! Let's pray as one young girl: "Our Father, which art in heaven, that's all I want."

Extra for Adults

A few days earlier the disciples were in Capernaum and were arguing about who would be greatest in the kingdom of heaven. Jesus knew of their discussion; and after asking them what they were talking about, Jesus brought a child before them. Read what Jesus said in Mark 9:36, 37. Isn't it interesting that the disciples seemed to forget this teaching as recorded in Matthew 18:3, 4?

Extra for Kids

Have you ever been left out of a game your friends were playing? It's disappointing not to get picked to be on a team, isn't it? Sometimes kids miss out on overnights, camping trips and parties; but the good news for you is that you are on God's team. You will never be left out if you know Jesus as your Savior!

As We Pray

Let's ask God to:

1. Help us to recognize the real relationship a child can have with God.

2. Help us to exercise a child-like trust and faith in Him as we live this life.

3. Your own prayer(s):

If you don't know Jesus as your Savior, but in your heart you want to, pray:

> Lord, I am a sinner. I am sorry for my sins. Please forgive me. I am turning away from my old life, and I am turning to You by trust and faith in You. I believe you died on the cross for me. Thank you for being my Savior.

Whoever believes in the Son has eternal life,
but whoever rejects the Son will not see life,
for God's wrath remains on him.
– John 3:36

22

Jerusalem News Services Flash Report: "Huge Crowd in Trouble"

"We have a problem here!"

"Jesus said, 'You feed them.' 'But we have only five loaves of bread and two fish,' they answered. 'Or are you expecting us to go and buy enough food for this whole crowd?' For there were about 5,000 men there."

— Luke 9:13, 14 (*NLT*)

You will enjoy reading the entire story found in Luke 9:10-17. It is hard for us to do so, but imagine we had never heard the account of the feeding of the 5,000 as recorded in the gospels. One thing for sure, the disciples had not faced anything like this before. A crowd of 5,000 men, plus women and children, had followed Jesus to a desert region near the town of Bethsaida.

My wife and I one time visited Quartzsite, Arizona, and as part of our experience took our camper van out into the desert. As softies we felt quite leery camping in a remote place even though we had food, water and a roof over our heads. The multitudes' physical situation was far more dangerous than ours. Since the disciples were not able to eat because of the press of people, Jesus led them to a solitary place for rest (Mark 6:31). It was in this remote desert region that the multitude followed Him, and with compassion the Lord again taught them and healed the sick.

But the hard conditions of the desert surroundings began to loom larger in the minds of the disciples, and late in the afternoon they became alarmed. They were actually quite direct with Jesus as they stepped up to take charge of the likely hunger crises. "*...Send the crowds away ... so they can find food and lodging*" (Luke 9:12 *NLT*). I do not fault the disciples for their concern. This was a caring response. One theologian suggested that since Jesus had created a great stir in Jerusalem and if a disaster occurred among His followers in the desert, Jesus and His disciples would be blamed.

> The advice of the disciples was owing to their fear that, as darkness would soon creep over the scene, some calamity might happen which would give a fresh handle against Jesus to His many enemies.[4]

I wonder what was going through their minds as they followed Jesus' instructions to have the people sit down in groups of 50 (verse 14), and when Jesus Himself took the five loaves and two fish, "*looked up to heaven, and blessed them*" (verse16). And what thoughts were going through their hearts and minds as "*they all ate as much as they wanted*" and as they were picking up 12 baskets of leftovers?! (See verse 17.) Let me tell you what I am thinking ... there is **no one** like this Jesus who so wisely taught them, who loved that mixed group of people, who brought them healing, who prayed with them and then demonstrated even another divine touch by multiplying the food so that they had more than enough to eat.

Have you ever noticed how much of our ministry as believers seems to happen in difficult settings? Sometimes the loss of loved ones takes place at nearly the same time as a wedding or another celebration. Illness might come when we begin a vacation.

The Apostle John explained in his gospel that Jesus asked Philip where they should buy bread for all the people "*only to test him, for he already had in mind what he was going to do*" (John 6:6).

Sometimes in ministry the electric power goes out, materials don't arrive or the key speaker is delayed. As we trust God, good things do happen. Once a terrible tornado hit a Bible camp that I managed. Staff and campers were huddled in a basement. I was actually gone that week, but the pastor in charge said, "I never had a prayer meeting as fervent as that one!" As believers, let's trust Him during times when the challenge is beyond our ability.

The feeding of the 5,000 was but a foretaste of another, far greater provision: that Jesus would provide a sacrifice for our sins. Thoughtfully and reverently, John later wrote these words:

John 1:14 (KJV) – "*The Word was made flesh and dwelt among us.*"

1 John 3:16 – "*Jesus Christ laid down his life for us.*"

1 John 5:11 – "*God has given us eternal life.*"

If you desire in your heart to know Jesus as your Savior, please go to the back of this book and read "Steps to Peace with God." They will help you to understand how to know Him as your Savior.

Extra for Adults

One reason we refer to the synoptic gospels as Matthew, Mark and Luke is because they often recorded the same events. Notice that John also recorded this miracle of the feeding of the 5,000 (John 6:1-15). See also Matthew 14:13-21, Mark 6:30-44 and Luke 9:10-17. From John 6 notice the response and the plan of the crowd after the meal was finished (John 6:14, 15). Why do you think Jesus slipped away?

Extra for Kids

Have you ever been to a potluck where the more the people ate, the more food there was at the table? Or at a dinner when your favorite foods NEVER disappeared? In Jesus' time the disciples had a lot more "cleanup duties" (Luke 9:17) than they had "set up" duties for the food in the first place! (See verse 16.) Who said they should pick up the food so none was wasted?

If you can find a map of Jesus' time, see if you can find the town of Bethsaida, where the feeding took place. Hint: find the top part of the Sea of Galilee.

As We Pray

1. Thank God for the provision of food that we need and enjoy.

2. Thank God for clearly recorded miracles that show how the same God of creation has control over natural things.

3. Pray that the recorded Bible miracles won't be brushed away like folklore by those close to us, our church and best friends. Pray that the Holy Spirit will use miracles to touch people's hearts for the Lord.

4. Pray for some people on your heart who don't know Jesus as Savior that God would speak to their heart and that they will receive Him as their Savior!

5. Your own prayer(s):

[4] H. D. M. Spence. *The Pulpit Bible Commentary on Luke, Vol. 16.* Grand Rapids: Eerdmans (1978), 234.

"*Do not let your hearts be troubled. Trust in God; trust also in me*" [Jesus].
– John 14:1

23

Forest, Rocks, Rivers and Flocks Join in Praise to God!

"Some of the Pharisees in the crowd said to Jesus, 'Teacher, rebuke your disciples!' 'I tell you,' he replied, 'If they keep quiet, the stones will cry out.'" **— Luke 19:39, 40**

What was the setting that led Jesus to declare the rocks would cry out? Read the fuller text in Luke 19:28-40.

Jesus had taught with authority, performed miracles before their eyes and ministered to them with love. When He came in humility on a donkey toward Jerusalem, the people placed their cloaks on the road before Him and soon praised Him as a King who came in the "*name of the Lord*" (verse 38).

Mindful of all the miracles Jesus had performed, they began to cry out: "*Blessed is the king who comes in the name of the Lord! Peace in heaven and glory in the highest!*" (verse 38).

The Pharisees and skeptics were troubled in part because they felt Jesus had bypassed them. They were jealous, especially when Jesus had accepted the people's praise of God's choice for King.

Can't you just hear them with indignation saying to Jesus, "*Rebuke your disciples*"? It was then that Jesus replied, "*If they* [the people] *keep quiet, the stones will cry out*" (verses 39, 40).

You may not have heard a preacher pose the question, "Could the stones ***really*** cry out?" Let's take a moment to look at this. Observe with me that the Bible has several participants in what we could call "Nature's Praise Orchestra and Choir" or simply "Nature's Praise Team"! May I present to you the members of this cast?

1. The flocks of sheep and fields of grain **sing** (Psalm 65:13).
2. The sea and all who live in it **shout** for joy (Psalm 98:7 *NLT*).
3. Rivers **clap** their hands, mountains **sing** for joy (Psalm 98:8).
4. Great sea creatures, hail, snow and clouds, stormy winds, mountains, all hills, fruit and cedar trees, wild animals and cattle, small creatures and flying birds, along with princes, young men and maidens, old men and children (and others)—these all **praise** or **sing** to the Lord!

Incidentally, on a sour note—house stones and beams cry out because of injustice (Habakkuk 2:11), and nature groans as with pains of childbirth (Romans 8:22).

Some of our readers may think I need to take a hermeneutics 101 class. But may I finally note that man was created from dust, and man can praise God quite nicely. But, enough already!

All of nature praises God with its beauty and intricacy. The metaphors are rich and powerful as they point to God's greatness, power and magnificence! The words from Jesus' mouth regarding the "*stones crying out*" herald the event of the very Son of God presenting Himself to Jerusalem and the world. He was both Savior and King! To those who trust in Him, He is the gift of love, an "*indescribable gift,*" who has come to redeem sinful men (2 Corinthians 9:15).

Simeon did not miss it while in the temple. As he held Jesus, he praised God saying, "*Now I can die content ... I have seen the Savior*" (Luke 2:29, 31 *TLB*). Anna, also in the Jerusalem temple, didn't miss the divine gift. She spread the happy news that "*the Messiah had finally arrived*" (Luke 2:38 *TLB*). The Apostle John didn't miss it, for he wrote years afterward: "*The Word* [Christ] *was made flesh and dwelt among us*" (John 1:14 *KJV*). But the Pharisees and skeptics missed it. You could say the people's praise kept the stones from crying out!

As believers in Christ, have we missed some of the wonderment of who God is and what He has done—that God left the splendor of heaven to enter the sinful world of man? It is perhaps not hard to slide into a routine of not thinking about God's great gift to us—even when we pray in Jesus' name. The busy issues of home life can choke a family's praise of God. Sometimes there is so much stuff going on at church that it can be hard to praise Him thoughtfully—even when we sing in church.

Thinking deeply about Jesus, Charles Wesley wrote the title and words in a hymn:

> *And can it be ... He left His Father's throne above ... emptied Himself of all but love, and bled for Adam's helpless race ... Amazing love! ... how can it be?*

And Jesus said, "*If they keep quiet, the stones will cry out*" (Luke 19:40).

Let's keep our sense of joyful wonder at the coming of God in the flesh. **This is one place where the word "awesome" fits!**

Extra for Adults

1. Revelation 19 has been described as a prophetic pageant. This passage speaks of human history as it is coming to a close. As you read the passage, notice the exuberance of the voices of praise in verses 1-8.

2. Read verses 11-16, thinking about the same Jesus who said to the Pharisees, "*If they keep quiet, the stones will cry out*" (Luke 19:40). This is the same Jesus that in His first coming came meekly on a donkey, but with so much love He laid down His life!

Extra for Kids

Have you ever felt small? I have felt small sometimes because so many people are smarter than me. Are you able to ride a 26" mountain bike? If not, you probably look forward to the day you are taller. Can you reach the top cupboard in your kitchen? Just with a stool maybe?

Guess what!? God loves small people. Jesus even went to a small man and said He wanted to go to his house (Luke 19:1-6)! I have a special verse for you today. It's Revelation 19:5: "*Then a voice came from the throne, saying: 'Praise our God, all you his servants, you who fear him, both small and great!'*" The God and Creator of all the universe wants your praise (Psalm 8:2). You are important! God bless you, small person!

As We Pray

1. Begin your time by moving from the "need" to praise Him to "actually" praising Him. If you would like, let the Psalmist lead you. If those are your heart thoughts in Psalm 119:173-175, praise Him with the Psalmist.

2. From your own heart would you think of ten things for which to praise Him.

3. Ask God to help you to not be distracted from praising Him as we live in this busy time.

4. If you wish, pray this prayer: "Lord, so many people publically use your name in profanity. Help me not to be shy to speak your name publically in praise!"

5. Your own prayer(s):

"*Yet to all who received him, to those who believed in his name, he gave the right to become children of God.*" – John 1:12

24

"Many Told Us, But We Did Not Hear It"

The Apostles

"He isn't here! He is risen from the dead! ... But the story sounded like nonsense to the men, so they didn't believe it ... As he spoke, he showed them his hands and his feet. Still they stood there in disbelief."

— Luke 24:6, 11, 40, 41 (*NLT*)

Please read the fuller text in Luke 24:33-43.

It is a reasonable question to ask, "Why did so many key believers, including the apostles, not seem to hear, anticipate or even believe for some time in the face of clear evidence that Jesus had risen from the dead?" Some have said they simply found Jesus' resurrection to be too great to comprehend. After studying the other gospels, some would say with a theologian named Spence that the apostles were simply in "wondering ecstasy."[5] Yet Mary Magdalene, with several prominent women who witnessed the empty tomb, told the apostles of their encounter with two angels who told them, "**He [Jesus] is risen!**" (Mark 16:6). The text says, "*They* [the apostles] *did not believe the women*" (Luke 24:11). Nor did the apostles believe the two eyewitness disciples who were on their way to Emmaus and had returned to Jerusalem (Mark 16:12). Then when Jesus showed the apostles His hands and feet, "*they still did not believe it*" (Luke 24:41).

We often think of one of the apostles as "doubting Thomas." But Thomas believed when he saw the scars on Jesus' body, for he said, "*My Lord and my God!*" (John 20:28). Yet the other apostles saw the same marks on our Savior and did not believe!

The Psalmist spoke of Jesus' resurrection: "*...nor will you let your Holy One see decay*" (Psalm 16:10). Jesus Himself made clear the coming events of His death and resurrection after three days.

> *From that time on Jesus began to explain to his disciples that he must go to Jerusalem ... and that he must be killed and on the third day be raised to life.* — Matthew 16:21

Somehow the apostles had also gotten distracted from the central truths of God's mission as Jesus indicated when He spoke to them: "*How foolish you are, and how slow of heart to believe all that the prophets have spoken! Did not the Christ have to suffer these things and then enter his glory?*" (Luke 24:25, 26).

Remarkably the enemies of our Savior heard, remembered and acted on Jesus' promise to be raised from the dead:

The next day, on the Sabbath, the leading priests and Pharisees went to see Pilate. They told him, "Sir, we remember what that deceiver once said while he was still alive: After three days I will rise from the dead..." (Matthew 27:62, 63 *NLT*).

The Pharisees had miscalculated events around Jesus before, and in their frail way they wanted Pilate to make sure no notoriety of any sort would come from the One they had gotten rid of.

Pilate gave them permission to seal the tomb and post guards. The seal was made up of a cord strung across the stone, which covered the tomb entrance. Clay was used to seal the cord at both ends. But in the minds of the priests and Pharisees, the real security to keeping Jesus' body in the tomb was the soldiers posted at the tomb entrance. The priests and Pharisees failed to understand that a cord, clay, stone, guards or any of man's efforts **would not keep the Son of God from rising from the dead!**

There is one thing we should keep in mind. The apostles and disciples, as well as the women of faith near Jesus, were extraordinary servants of Christ. While they failed to see the reality of the coming death and resurrection in the early years of ministry, they gave up careers and comforts as they followed Christ's call. Often as they proclaimed Christ, they were beaten and withstood opposition to the death. We need to see them in the context of their whole lives of faith and sacrifice!

Why is the resurrection of Christ important to us today? While this incredible subject merits much study and application, there are three important realities of the resurrection of Christ.

The ***first*** is that **God keeps His word**. 2 Peter 3:9 (*KJV*) says, "*The Lord is not slack concerning his promise.*" The resurrection of Christ was the fulfillment of a divine promise. Committing ourselves to the truth that God keeps His promises can sustain us in times of strain and doubt. Our faith will be rewarded as we trust in Him for whatever He promised.

Δ

What God promised leads us to a ***second*** important truth of the resurrection. **Jesus Christ has the power over death.** During the terrible drought of the 1930s in the central U.S., some *rainmakers* would show up to give people hope. Those who endured those terrible dry storms of sand and dirt were told they only needed to have faith in the rainmakers. The problem was that no rain fell on the dry land.

Our faith needs to be grounded in the One who created life, who sent Jesus to die for our sins and who has demonstrated His power over death. To raise the dead is the business of the One who created us in the beginning. All four gospel writers wanted us to get that message, and all four recorded the resurrection of Jesus Christ! Later the Apostle Paul said, "*God will raise us up from the dead by his power, just as he raised our Lord from the dead*" (1 Corinthians 6:14 *NLT*).

The resurrection of Jesus Christ is important because God kept His promise, He has the power, and ***third,* we have a durable hope** to carry us through the low and high points of this life. The Apostle Peter moved from bewilderment at the news of the resurrection to boldly proclaiming it:

> *Praise be to the God and Father of our Lord Jesus Christ! In his great mercy he has given us new birth into a living hope through the resurrection of Jesus Christ from the dead, and into an inheritance that can never perish, spoil or fade – kept in heaven for you.* — 1 Peter 1:3, 4

What a promise! What power! What hope! This miracle is ours to enjoy and proclaim and to live and die with. God bless you as you treasure ***the resurrection*** of Jesus and the promise of ours to come. If you are not sure you will be resurrected into heaven and you want to know, see "Steps to Peace with God" at the back of the book. This will help you to become sure.

Extra for Adults

Read Revelation 1:4-18, noting this vision of the living and glorified Christ. Notice the vision the Apostle John had of Jesus in verses 12-16. Remember, this is the same Jesus who meekly rode on the foal of a donkey and said that He could call out for "*twelve legions of angels*" to deliver Him from the mob at Gethsemane (Matthew 26:53). Notice, also, how He refers to the events of His death and resurrection in Revelation 1:18. May we all be encouraged that we have our trust in the One who is our eternal God with the power over death.

Extra for Kids

When I was a kid, I loved to watch Zorro on TV. This hero of the black and white screen would swoop down with his black horse, black hat, black mask and black cape upon communities of poor Mexican people, who were being abused by powerful rulers. There was no end to his retrieving justice, stolen property and kidnapped damsels in distress. (If you don't know what a damsel in distress is, ask an adult.) As humans, even little humans, we want a joyful and hopeful life; and Zorro (my TV hero) was it!

A problem came up. One time Zorro didn't show up. I couldn't believe it. The gold, the good mayor and the girl were all lost. Zorro apologized. What!? The horse got sick? "Don't apologize, Zorro, do your rescue job!" The final episode was "To Be Continued," but the next week I had to go to a piano recital. I think I would have been horrified to watch the end of the Zorro story. Maybe my "hero" would mess up again!

Our heroes in this life, both fictional and real, will sometimes disappoint and fail us. But as we go through good times and hard times, the Bible encourages us by saying, "*The Lord is near to all who call on him ... The Lord watches over all who love him*" (Psalm 145:18, 20). God bless you as you trust the One who gave us life and raised Jesus from the dead! **He will not fail**!

As We Pray

1. Praise the Lord with the Apostle Peter as God gave us a new birth into a living hope through His resurrection.

2. Ask God to give us strength in our latter days of life to not fear death but to be comforted by the promise of eternal life.

3. Ask God to help us to keep a thirst and hunger for God's Word.

4. Ask God to help us to show our life's hope in Christ to others in our expressions, what we say and what we do.

5. Your own prayer(s):

[5] H. D. M. Spence. *The Pulpit Commentary on Luke, Vol. 16*. Grand Rapids: Eerdmans (1978), 274.

25

Disciples Grumble, "We Quit!"

"Then said Jesus unto the twelve, 'Will ye also go away?' Then Simon Peter answered him, 'Lord, to whom shall we go?'"

— John 6:67, 68 (*KJV*)

In some ways this had been an exhilarating time for the disciples. The crowds had swollen as Jesus fed 5,000 people, walked on water and healed the sick. The disciples were near the center of these miraculous displays of Jesus' power. Please read a fuller text in John 6:53-69.

An unexpected potential road block had come before the disciples as Jesus spoke of the need to eat His flesh and drink His blood as a path to eternal life. The Master Teacher's statement dismayed many followers. Even the faithful grumbled, "*This is a hard teaching. Who can accept it?*" (verse 60).

What did Peter do in that perplexing moment? I believe Peter drew from all he knew about the Master's powerful deeds and teaching to know that this Jesus, whether he always understood or not, was the Christ, the anointed One of God. Peter might have thought about the testimonies and actions of the Savior. Today if we had time to ponder the question, we might rehearse quite a few reasons to believe Jesus is the Christ. The Old Testament prophets, among them Isaiah, laid out messianic descriptions that were fulfilled in Jesus. The shepherds and astrologers confirmed Jesus as the Savior King. When in the temple with Jesus, Simeon and Anna affirmed that He was the Savior. Jesus Himself said, "*The miracles I do in my Father's name speak for me*" (John 10:25). Today we have the testimony of the gospel writers and other New Testament authors who clearly identify Jesus as God's Son and our redeemer.

When Jesus spoke of eating His flesh and drinking His blood, this was not literal; but the larger group of disciples and the Twelve did not understand. The meaning later became clear as the New Testament writers themselves used similar imagery. The moment, however, was tense and even somewhat bewildering to the disciples. God wanted them to have faith even when they struggled with His teaching. He wants us to have faith in Him as well, even though we don't understand everything about the Bible or life itself.

Note that when Jesus asked if Peter wanted to also leave Jesus' side, it was the Spirit of God deep in Peter's heart that quickly prompted him to say, "*Lord, to whom shall we go? You have the words of eternal life. We believe and know that you are the Holy One of God*" (John 6:68, 69).

If you do not understand some issues of your faith, please consider the blind man as recorded in John 9. After he received his sight, he clung to what he knew. Jesus gave him sight (verses 15, 25), Jesus was a prophet (verse 17), and becoming quite bold he gave the Pharisees a sermon they didn't want to hear (verses 30-33). That got the formerly blind man kicked out of the synagogue. Acting on what he knew—and not having all the understanding we seem to crave today—he said, "*Lord, I believe,*" and he "*worshipped*" Jesus (verse 38). That is what we need to do today: act on what understanding His Spirit has given us!

Like the faithful disciples, we are occasionally tested in our trust of Christ and in our ability to understand what God has said and what He is doing in the world around us. Even if the world's citizens abandon their Christianity in droves and the thought of leaving Jesus' side ever comes to us, as believers we are in Christ and His Spirit dwells in our very being. We, too, must say, "To whom would we go? He is my Savior!" **We might not understand all things every moment, but we know and cling to Christ by faith.** Soon enough we will come to understand. Blessings on you as your faith grows!

If you don't know and worship Jesus as the once blind man did and you want to know Him, go to "Steps to Peace with God" at the back of this book. It will help you.

Extra for Adults

Notice another passage that was hard for the disciples. They didn't get it. Read Mark 8:11-21: "The Case of the Bread Shortage?" Observe how they stay the course with Jesus, always learning and growing.

Extra for Kids

1. Go around the room and each of you describe the wind. Tell someone near you what it is. (Try this before you go to #2.)

2. Did you describe a color? A shape or a sound? Was that the wind? Not really.

Remember, some things about God are mysteries. A guy by the name of Nicodemus asked Jesus about His teachings. Please read John 3:3-9. Nicodemus did not understand how the Spirit comes to give a believer in Jesus a ***new birth.*** Also, He didn't know how a full-grown man could be born again. Think about that! But at some point he had life-changing faith. He was there to honor God by helping to take Jesus' body off the cross. Let's have faith in Jesus although we don't understand everything.

As We Pray

1. Pray we will continue as people of faith even though we sometimes don't understand all of the Bible.
2. Pray we will trust in the Lord with all our heart and will not lean on our own understanding (Proverbs 3:5, 6).
3. Pray for your pastor for health, wisdom, strength in God and joy in his ministry.
4. Your own prayer(s):

26

Worms Eat god

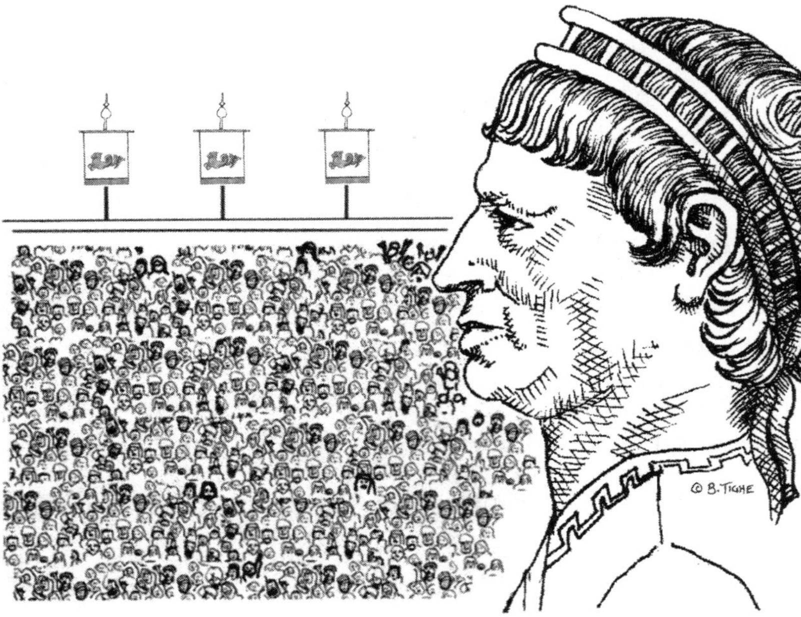

"This is not the voice of a man, but of a god; not a man, not a man, of a god, of a god!"

"When the day arrived, Herod put on his royal robes, sat on his throne, and made a speech to them. The people gave him a great ovation, shouting, 'It's the voice of a god, not of a man!' Instantly, an angel of the Lord struck Herod with a sickness, because he accepted the people's worship instead of

giving the glory to God. So he was consumed with worms and died."

–Acts 12:21-23 (*NLT*)

Well, that was a fast narrative! If you missed it, it didn't take long for this pompous king to move from worship to worms! For a fuller text read Acts 12:20-23.

How did this all come to be? King Herod was quite a politician. He had made friends with Rome and the Jewish people to the extent that he ruled nearly all of the territory Herod the Great once ruled. To please the Jews further he set out to do harm to the Christians, having James, the brother of John, beheaded. Because such acts against the church made him popular with the Jews, he had Peter seized and imprisoned. Before he could have Peter slain, an angel came at night and freed him (Acts 12:1-3, 11).

This real-life drama continued when a very anxious trade delegation wanted an audience with King Herod Agrippa I. They wanted to talk to him about better food supplies for their hungry people back home. They came before the king alright, but Herod came dressed in his royal robes and decided it was a great time to give a kingly speech to a large group of subjects as well as to the delegation. He addressed the people and impressed the crowd, which included many loyal Jews, to the point where the people shouted, "*It's the voice of a god, not of a man!*" (verse 22).

In addition to pleasing his audience with words, Herod's appearance was dazzling. Some historians recorded that the king's robe was made almost entirely of glistening silver. Imagine the sparkle and flashing light that the people saw as the king spoke to them (verse 21).

Herod did not resist the worship directed to him. He did not redirect the people to the living God of Israel. Then God acted. An angel instantly struck Herod with illness, and he was eaten alive (likely from the inside out) and died. We read in Proverbs 16:18: "*Pride goes before destruction.*"

We live in a world today that often glorifies pride and arrogance in entertainment, sports, education and so-called "reality shows." Pride is often not subtle. God resists the proud but favors the humble (1Peter 5:5). Let us choose "*humble.*"

Δ

Note the warning of Malachi 4:1 (*KJV*):

> *For, behold, the day cometh, that shall burn as an oven; and all the proud, yea, and all that do wickedly, shall be stubble: and the day that cometh shall burn them up, saith the LORD of hosts, that it shall leave them neither root nor branch.*

The Apostle Paul warned believers that if we have stature (usually wealth, position or family) and we are with people of low estate, we should not be proud. "*Live in harmony with each other. Don't be too proud to enjoy the company of ordinary people. And don't think you know it all!*" (Romans 12:16 *NLT*).

Let's resist the proud influences and embrace the Apostle James' thoughts: "*Humble yourselves before the Lord, and he will lift you up*" (James 4:10).

An example of humility is from a child who resisted pride and did something surprising. An Awana ministry we served encouraged children to memorize Scripture so they would know the God and counsel of the Bible. Providing extra motivation was the earning of "Awana bucks," which allowed the children to purchase gifts for others or prizes for themselves. One eight-year-old boy was memorizing many times more verses than other children. I noticed he always had a gentle smile whenever the Monopoly®-like Awana bucks were passed out to him in amounts many times greater than the other clubbers. Never did he give a hint of conceit, bragging or pride as he continued to heap his fortune away in his clubber bag. Toward the end of the year he asked to speak to the leaders and clubbers about his small fortune. "I would like to make a suggestion," he said. "Since I have more Awana bucks than I need, would it be OK for me to give some to others who have so few?" The lesson is for us as well. It seems real humility is coupled with generosity!

Let's resist pride, give God the praise, humble ourselves and be generous.

Extra for Adults

Read the account of the centurion of Luke 7:1-10. We often cite the great faith of this centurion. Is not his humility equally remarkable and an example to us? Proverbs 21:4 says, "*Haughty eyes and a proud heart ... are sin!*" Isn't it interesting that pride can be seen in someone's eyes?

Extra for Kids

Hey, kids. I bet you hear some friends say stuff like: "I'm the fastest runner, I have more toys than you or I have an iPhone and you don't." That kind of talk is proud and braggin'-type stuff, right? How can we talk better to please God? How about, "I like my bike; but I like yours, too!" "You have nice tennis shoes; but I am happy with mine, too!" "My best fun is with good friends."

You can help think of some:

____

____

____

____

As We Pray

1. Does Psalm 115:1 (*NLT*) reflect your heart? If this is where your heart is, pray that prayer: "*Not to us, O Lord, not to us, but to your name goes all the glory for your unfailing love and faithfulness.*"

2. Ask God for His Spirit to work in your life to help you to reflect the humility God intends.

3. Ask Him also to use you to touch others that others would see in you an example of strength and humility.

4. Pray that others would be uplifted by your living testimony.

5. Your own prayer(s):

"Then Jesus declared, 'I am the bread of life. He who comes to me will never go hungry, and he who believes in me will never be thirsty.'" —John 6:35

27

Guarding Your Hearts and Minds

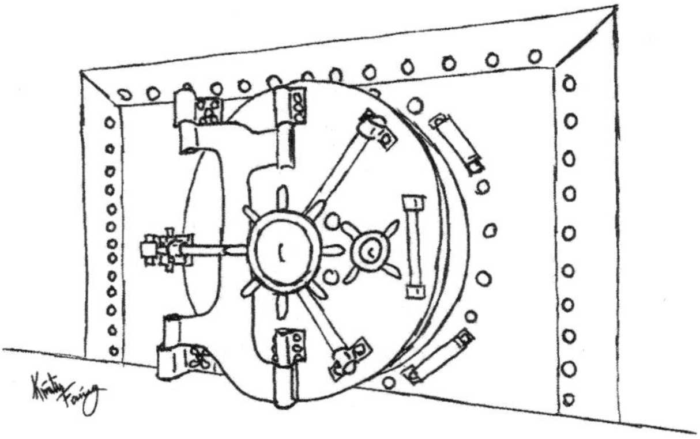

"Do not be anxious about anything, but in everything, by prayer and petition, with thanksgiving, present your requests to God. And the peace of God, which transcends all understanding, will guard your hearts and your minds in Christ Jesus."

— Philippians 4:6, 7

Several financial experts regarded the Diamond Center in Antwerp, Belgium, as the absolute safest in the world. It was equipped with ten layers of security, including Doppler radar, seismic sensors and motion detectors. In addition, the lock had 100 million likely combinations. It was a major center for the precious jewels of the world, and the designers and managers of the Diamond Center took great measures to keep the treasures safe. In spite of the security system, on February 22, 2003, thieves broke in and stole most of the valuable stones, hauling off about $100 million in jewels. The safe and all the security failed to guard the treasure!

Our hearts and minds are far more valuable than earthly jewels. What makes them so valuable? From our hearts flow love, passion and emotion. With our minds we receive data, analyze, form judgments and make decisions. To some Bible scholars and philosophers, the heart is the seat of the mind. The heart will set a pattern for how the mind will work. As believers we want God's holy values to shape our hearts and minds, and we are to guard them. How do we do that?

The safety and security of our hearts and minds are found in three truths in Philippians 4:6, 7. The passage begins with the ***first truth*** and counsel: "**Do not be anxious about anything.**" Anxiety can come from temptation, illness, finances, jobs, relationships and a whole bunch of things.

One cause of worry is simply being too busy. Consider this office scene: A CEO of a fairly large firm was making a rare and hurried appearance though the company's office center. A diligent office worker spotted him and saw her chance. Speeding over to the aisle before him she said, "Pardon me sir, may I ask you just one thing?" The busy chief executive listened and answered the question as best he could. Then looking around the bustling room he said, "Madam, may I ask you just one question: which way was I going when you stopped me?"

With the demands on our time, it seems many of us are on overload. Sometimes our anxiety comes from careless over-planning.

The ***second truth*** from verse six is: "**By prayer and petition, with thanksgiving, present your requests to God.**" This is more than merely asking Him for help.

Going to Him with thanksgiving is a sign of faith that our Lord is in control. Trusting in Him leads to great security!

Our worry will not guard our inward treasure of Jesus, nor will human positive thinking; however, looking to Him with absolute trust will lead to a divine peace from God that will in turn place His lock of protection on our hearts and minds.

The security measures are now in place. By not being anxious and by trusting God who is in control, we are secure. The ***third truth*** of the passage is great news: "*And* **the peace of God**, *which transcends all understanding,* **will guard your hearts and your minds in Christ Jesus**" (verse seven). This comes by knowing that God is in absolute control and by having complete dependence upon Him. No one can break in and steal the treasure of Jesus in your heart and mind with this security system!

Extra for Adults

Read Luke 10:38-42. How can we adjust our thinking and behavior to reflect Mary's choices and Jesus' affirmation of her?

Observe the progression. Our tendency toward anxiety → our thankful prayers and requests → peace of God = guarded hearts and minds.

Extra for Kids

Sometimes we have fears that seem very hard or almost impossible to fix. But you **can** look to heaven and tell your problems to Him. Check a box after you have told God your problem and asked Him for help.

☐ ☐ ☐ ☐ ☐ ☐

You are secure and safe if you trust Him!

As We Pray

1. Pray that we will try not to go it alone for solving our troubles.

2. Pray that we won't be anxious but trusting in Him.

3. Pray that we will sense God's protection of our hearts to love and our minds to think clearly on the issues of each day.

4. Your own prayer(s):

28

It Is with Great Pleasure I Present. . .

(Part 1)

"God's chosen people, holy and dearly loved." — Colossians 3:12

Have you ever been introduced to a large group of people? Perhaps you were about to give a report, talk about your life or speak to an audience looking for inspiration or information. If I were coming to the podium, I would be tempted to speak some words expressing humility. Perhaps I would set out to diminish any lofty description of myself.

If you have placed your faith in Christ Jesus as the Apostle Paul made clear to his readers in Colossians 1:4, you have just been presented as **chosen**, **holy** and **dearly loved**. If Jesus is your Savior, write your names on the following blank spaces:

May I Present: ________________ ________________

________________ ________________ ________________

________________ ________________ ________________

These are "*God's chosen people, holy and dearly loved*"! (Colossians 3:12). This description might lead you to pause or feel embarrassed for the proud words chosen. But that is you if you are in Christ. Exhilarating? I say, "Yes!"

You are chosen. The Apostle Peter wrote to several scattered believers downtrodden by their culture, largely because of persecution: "*You are a chosen people*" (1 Peter 2:9). Isn't it impressive that God has given forethought and favor to you in His plan?

In addition to choosing you and because of the work of Jesus, He has made you "**holy and blameless** *as you stand before Him without a single fault*" (Colossians 1:22 *NLT*). Can this fit me? You? Think about this: if we are prosecuted in a court of law for several crimes and the judge declares us "not guilty" of all charges, we are free from all the charges just as if we had never been accused. In the same way, God as judge has declared us blameless because of Christ's work on the cross and our repentance and faith. In his letter to the Philippians, Paul said it this way: "*...not having a righteousness of my own that comes from the law, but that which is through faith in Christ*" (Philippians 3:9).

We are also **dearly loved**. In his crusades, Billy Graham would repeat the phrase "God loves you" several times, and many in the audience were touched by the message of this love from heaven. Imagine the Creator as being a lover of you and me! The Apostle John said, "*This is how we know what love is: Jesus Christ laid down his life for us*" (1 John 3:16).

In Christ we are chosen, holy and dearly loved. Do you like the Bible description of you? I do. If you are hesitant to accept the uplifting words, remember that it is God's work in you. It is by His grace and power that this truth is realized.

If this description simply doesn't fit you, or you are unsure if you know Jesus as your Savior, would you go to "Steps to Peace with God" in the back of this book? This may help you to find Christ as your personal Savior.

Extra for Adults

1. Are we chosen, holy and loved even when we sin? See Romans 5:8; 8:28-39; and Ephesians 2:4, 5.

2. A phrase often quoted a few years ago was "Please be patient, God is not finished with me yet." While we are presently "*chosen, holy and dearly loved*" in His sight today, see what He has for us in the future (1 John 3:2).

Extra for Kids

Know that we are "*chosen, holy, and dearly loved,*" but we are not conceited or bragging when we say that. This description comes from God. Do you think God might change His mind about you? There is a passage that says you are special, and He won't change His mind. Look up Romans 8:38, 39. That's good news!

As We Pray

1. Pray that as believers we would have the proper self-esteem that God desires us to have: chosen, holy, and dearly loved.

2. Pray that God would give us the words to communicate to people without Christ so this can become their reality, too!

3. Pray that we would enjoy our place in God's family and also be on guard to abide in Him.

4. Your own prayer(s):

29

Presenting...
Grouchy vs. Lovely
(Part 2)

"Clothe yourselves ... put on love."

— Colossians 3:12

"A happy heart makes the face cheerful, but heartache crushes the spirit."

— Proverbs 15:13

I would like to tell you a story about Tom. Occasionally he is a "stick-in-the-mud." A Valentine's Day dinner and program was coming up at church. He said he'd go but was disgruntled that he would be missing a well-publicized sports event on TV. He rationalized somehow that going to this event celebrating red hearts and stuff was proof of his undying love and clear dedication to his wife. But he still found it hard to shake off his grumpies about the whole matter. "Who schedules a Valentine event on February 14 when there is a major semi-final sports event?" he said.

Folks at his church had put a lot of work into this Valentine's program. Songs, readings, stories and a Bible time followed the dinner. Colorful visuals decorated the walls and tables. All generations of the church were invited.

On the morning of the event Tom thought he felt a little cold coming on. "If this got worse," he thought, "this would be a sign; it wouldn't be fair to expose all those people to my germs!" But alas, later on Tom was fine.

By late afternoon Tom was planning for the Valentine event. After setting the TV recorder to capture the sports action, Tom gave the edict, "Whatever you do, don't tell me the outcome before I get a chance to watch it." Tom noticed that his wife had already been preparing herself for the Valentine's program and that she looked very nice. He chuckled, thinking that perhaps she was overdoing it a little bit.

Tom decided to ditch his oil change clothes for something cleaner, and after cleaning up he slipped on a favorite shirt and comfortable jeans. His wife stopped him in the hallway. "You're not wearing that, I hope!" she said. He was a little stunned; that golf shirt had been his favorite for six years! The jeans were hardly faded! "You know folks don't dress up at church like they used to. OK," he said in a feigned dramatic submission. "You put out the clothes you want me to wear." Upon his return to the bedroom, Tom found blue dress slacks and his nicest dress shirt on the bed, along with a bright red tie he never wore.

When arriving at church, Tom discovered a genuine festive atmosphere. He was surprised to see his sports buddies there. As it turned out, Tom had a very good time. The tone of the evening deepened as the pastor spoke on 1 Corinthians 13, the love chapter. Tom became taken up with the whole celebration of love and the ending focus on God's love. A buddy had run out to his car, come back and blurted out the sporting results; but it didn't bother him. He went home fed, encouraged and blessed.

You might wonder why I told this story about Tom. How does this Valentine's Day experience fit in with Colossians 3:12,14?

The answer is this: **God loves you and wants to dress you up**! The Colossians 3:12-17 directives given by God through the Apostle Paul are clothes from a very classy wardrobe as a reflection of God's love for us. Unlike Tom's attitude toward dressing up for a special person and event, we need to have a happy heart and cheerfully let God choose our clothes **because we love Him in return**!

Being disgruntled about circumstances around us and harboring a grumpy attitude will simply keep God's best from us. Before He clothes us (Part 3), let's be joyful that He wants to bring about the best things in our life. Let the Psalmist's praise be ours: "*I will be glad and rejoice in you*" (Psalm 9:2).

The bottom line? It's not hard to accommodate or dress up for someone you love. The obedience of putting on certain clothes for God should flow from our love for Him. As His "**dearly loved**," we draw from the awareness that we have come to love **Him** dearly. "*We love him, because he first loved us*" (1 John 4:19 *KJV*). God bless you as you serve Him cheerfully and lovingly, realizing that by doing so He has a wonderful plan of blessing for you. In Part 3 we will see the kinds of clothing God has for us.

Extra for Adults

1. Being as candid as you can, what motivates you to:
   a. Read the Bible?
   b. Pray?
   c. Fellowship with the church?
   d. Serve the Lord with the abilities He gave you?

2. Consider the words of Mary in response to God's plan for her in Luke 1:38.

Extra for Kids

1. What types of clothes do you like the best?
2. What clothes do you hate to wear?
3. Do you sometimes wear clothes because someone else wants you to wear them?
4. What kinds of things might you do because you want to please God while friends do something else?
5. Get ready to put on clothes that God wants you to wear. 1 Samuel 12:24 might help.

As We Pray

1. Tell God that you love Him.
2. Ask God for help to have a good heart attitude toward the Lord as He wants to dress us up.
3. Pray for people who come to mind who may have a hard time seeing God's love.
4. Your own prayer(s):

30

Presenting...
God's Wardrobe for Me
(Part 3)

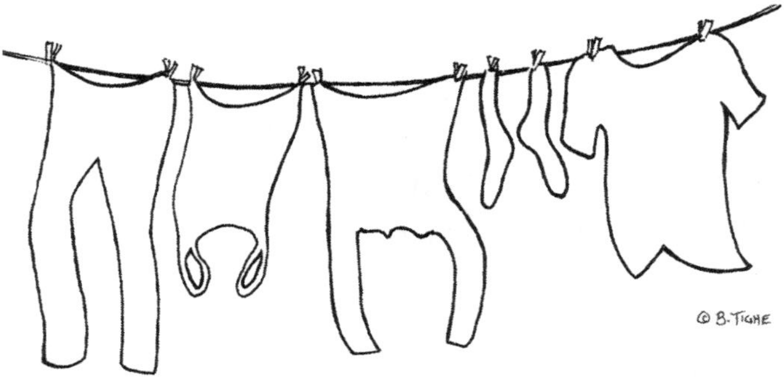

"Clothe yourselves with compassion, kindness, humility, gentleness and patience. Bear with each other and forgive whatever grievances you may have against one another. Forgive as the Lord forgave you. And over all these virtues put on love."

— Colossians 3:12-14

In Part 1 of this three-part series, we focused on the Apostle Paul's teaching that we are "*chosen, holy and dearly loved*" by God. Part 2 pointed to the need for us to love God in return. That love for God will lead us to be willing to let Him clothe us as He desires, knowing that God's plans will bring the very best of blessings to us. With that preparation, let's look at what the clothing is.

Read Colossians 3:12-17 twice, imagining wearing these virtues.

The words attached to the clothing we are to wear are of the most noble and godly character. Before we offer a brief description below of the five qualities, first look at each one listed in verse 12 and note your own impressions of what each is like, starting with compassion.

Let's look at the five in verse 12, comparing our impressions:

1. ***Compassion***—Some liken this to pity, but for sure it is a deep heart feeling for people especially for those suffering.

2. ***Kindness***—This has the idea of a pleasant dealing with others. It has been called "sweet service to people."

3. ***Humility***—A lowliness of mind, which keeps one's pride from getting in the way.

4. ***Gentleness***—A soft dealing with others; the opposite is harshness. Some scholars say it is not insisting on perfection.

5. ***Patience***—Being tireless in being supportive and helpful. The opposite would be resentment.

As a child I used to dream about being one of the members of the fabled Swiss Robinson family, who was forced to live on a tropical island after getting shipwrecked in the early 1800s. The novel, which was written in 1879, and English films produced in 1940 and 1960, captivated my thoughts for years as I imagined how wonderful it would be to live on that faraway island. But as I thought about it years later, it was not the island, beautiful beach, sunsets and living off the land that were attractive. It was the way the isolated family worked together that was so appealing to me. The fictional story had the characters on the island figuring things out together, happily discovering life, protecting each other, laughing with their work, making sure everyone was included and helping each other in trouble.

The virtues of caring for one another as the Apostle Paul exhorted in his letter to the Colossian believers are not the stuff of fiction. They were designed to be real. Perhaps you are part of a church that cares and serves one another and also that reflects the beauty of those five words. Perhaps not. Let's ask God to shape our hearts to make those words a reality.

Δ

A problem has arisen. When my heavenly Father and Savior tells me today to put on compassion, kindness, humility, gentleness and patience, I try—but it doesn't fit very well. I confess, "This isn't working!" Yes, I'm familiar with the clothing of Colossians 3:12-14. I experiment with putting on a kind of *papier mâché* version of the clothing, but alas the effort becomes futile within days. I am cordial and nice, civil and well-behaved; but in my heart there is a battle to do my Lord's bidding. Sometimes the compassion, kindness, humility, gentleness and patience have all but fallen off.

It is very hard to do these things for my heavenly Father, as I see them the same way I saw the "do list" of my earthly father. If Dad said, "Do it," I was brought up to do it. It got done, but my heart wasn't always in it. So also the putting on of these clothes without my heart being in it doesn't seem to work well for me, even though I have signed on.

But God gave the Apostle Paul the formula to make it work. It came in two parts. The ***first*** is in verse 13: "*Bear with each other and forgive whatever grievances you may have against one another. Forgive as the Lord forgave you.*" This hearkens back to our very salvation as God has forgiven us! God is saying to our hearts: forgive others. My progress to wear these clothes begins to move ahead as a result of a forgiving heart.

When I look back on my heart, sin, behavior and failures, I am amazed God has forgiven me. I don't want to be a hypocrite. I have been forgiven and need to forgive others with whom I may have grievances.

After pointing out clothes of great virtue, the Apostle Paul introduced a ***second*** part in Colossians 3:14. There he said above all: "*...put on love, which binds them all* [the five items of clothing] *together in perfect unity.*" G. G. Findlay wrote on this very passage years ago:

> [Love] is the substance of the Christian virtues ... here it is that which embraces and completes them. They [the virtues of Colossians 3:12-14] imply love, but it is more than them all together.[6]

Findlay went on to say that all the virtues "fall to pieces and are nothing"[7] without love. Findlay's point is right; sometimes our best human efforts "fall to pieces." The key is to put on love (3:14). Our love for God is tied together with our love for one another. Consider Jesus' words:

> *So now I am giving you a new commandment: Love each other. Just as I have loved you, you should love each other. Your love for one another will prove to the world that you are my disciples.* — John 13:34-35 (*NLT*)

That simply changes everything for me. It will for you, too. Forgiveness and love open the door for great things, and your heart will change!

I trust that as you know the love of God, you will also experience the binding effect of love, and in obedience love others around you. He will enable you to wear the clothes of compassion, kindness, humility, gentleness and patience.

You can be sure this apparel will look very nice on you. May God richly bless you as His Spirit works through your heart and as you step out with this clothing!

Extra for Adults

The "love chapter" is wonderful reading. Read 1 Corinthians 13 slowly and thoughtfully. The Apostle John wrote more about love than his fellow apostles. Read 1 John 5:1-5. What do you think is the connection between defeating the "*evil world*" and love?

Extra for Kids

We have a neighbor dog, which is about the ugliest mammal I have ever seen; yet the family's kids love him to death! Have you ever seen a kid love an ugly dog or other animal? I once saw a lady show her furless cat on TV. She really loved that cat!

We can love people who have an ugly way about them, such as a neighbor who does rude things. Jesus can teach us to love them as we let Him work in our hearts. Perhaps you can pick up their recycling bin, make some cookies for them or simply say "Good morning!" Remember people who love Jesus should have special love. Perhaps someone sits alone at church. Would you be brave and sit by them? Colossians 3:13 says to bear with each other (which means to overlook some things you don't like about them). Say, "Hi" or "Have a good day." How about praying for them—would you do these things? Please put your initials below if you will.

☐ ☐ ☐ ☐ ☐ ☐

As We Pray

1. Tell God that you love Him.
2. Pray that we will understand love better, first God's and then ours to Him and others.
3. Pray that God's love will lead you to new levels of compassion, kindness, humility, gentleness and patience.
4. Pray that as we step out with expressions of love everyone we love will sense God's Spirit through us and not think we want something for ourselves.
5. Your own prayer(s):

[6] G. G. Findlay. *The Pulpit Commentary on Colossians, Vol. 20*. Grand Rapids: Eerdmans (1977), 153.
[7] Ibid.

31

It's Come to This...

WANTED

Dead or Alive

"My People"

With My love, care
and promise

God

Eternal Reward!

***"He died for us so that, whether we are awake or asleep, we may live together with him."* — 1 Thessalonians 5:10**

Over my ministry years I have had the opportunity of being at the bedside of ill saints, many of whom were elderly. Several were aware that they were soon to pass on from their life on earth to a life with God. As I listened to many of them, it became clear that the promises of Scripture sealed their thinking and comfort. My expressions of love and care, as well as my reading of thoughtful Scripture passages, would be met by their sturdy testimony of salvation and anticipation of "going home." Often the "afflicted" ministered to the comforter, and I went away blessed.

Could these words of faithful believers have been merely lofty platitudes or the very ill putting forward their best face? After all, doesn't a religious person need to say the right things around others? This was certainly ***not*** the case! Steadfastly, they had taken God at His Word, quoting to me their favorite verses of promise. John 11:25-26, where Jesus said, "*I am the resurrection and the life. He who believes in me will live, even though he dies; and whoever lives and believes in me will never die,*" is one such verse believers have quoted.

Here is the bottom line. We are normally truly sorrowful in the loss of a loved one; sometimes when the death is unexpected, it cuts deeper than we can ever describe. The loss of Dorcas (Tabitha) as recorded in Acts 9:36-42 brought about many tears and open grief among those who loved her. The truth has been said many times that the loved one in Christ is "in a better place." But the place is not a vague cosmic space in the sky. It is certainly not true that the person is resting in peace buried at the grave site! The statement is correct because the "place" is at the side of Jesus, with the God and King who has been in charge of the world since creating it and who has planned your salvation. Read Colossians 1:15-20.

Jesus said to the repentant criminal dying on a cross next to Him: "*I tell you the truth, today you will be with me in paradise*" (Luke 23:43). The Apostle Paul wrote: "*Our citizenship is in heaven*" (Philippians 3:20). Your loved one in Christ is just where he or she should be! The Apostle Paul could with authority also say: "*I desire to depart and be with Christ, which is better by far!*" (Philippians 1:23).

If you are one who knows Jesus Christ as your Savior and you feel the time of your death is close, think about His promise that He is preparing a place for you in His house (John 14:1-3). Please read it. Take God's promise deep into your heart. Doing so will be of great comfort to you.

Extra for Adults

Please read Acts 9:36-43. How might this account relate to the future life promised us in respect to the power of God that worked through Peter?

Extra for Kids

1. Imagine being with Jesus someday when He brings the children who love Him to be close by Him in heaven.

2. Revelation 5:9-14 talks about singing in heaven. Imagine singing with tens of thousands of angels!

3. What song do you like now that you might like to sing in heaven? Did you know that sometimes there are new songs in heaven (verse 9)?

4. Do you think you will have a better voice?

As We Pray

1. Thank Him for being clear so we know that when we die, we are looked after eternally.

2. Pray for help to memorize and keep close to our heart the heaven promises of the Bible. (1 Peter 1:3 is a good example: "*He has given us new birth into a living hope...kept in heaven for you.*")

3. Ask Him to help us be willing and bold to share with people around us that they can be forgiven of their sins and have life with Jesus forever!

4. Pray for the teachers in your church.

5. Your own prayer(s):

Devotional Reader's Guide

#	Shorter Time	Longer Time	Δ	In a Series	Seasonal Days	Salvation Application	Date Read
1	X						
2	X						
3	X						
4	X						
5			X			X	
6	X					X	
7	X						
8			X				
9	X						
10	X						
11		X					
12	X				Christmas		
13		X					
14	X						
15	X						
16	X						
17	X						
18			X		Easter	X	
19			X				
20	X			X	Christmas		
21	X			X			
22		X				X	
23		X			Palm Sunday		
24			X		Easter	X	
25	X					X	
26		X					
27	X						
28	X			X		X	
29	X			X	Valentine's		
30			X	X			
31	X				Death		

Δ Indicates possible break in the case of a longer devotional. Reader has option of resuming at a later time.

STEPS TO PEACE WITH GOD

1. RECOGNIZE GOD'S PLAN—PEACE AND LIFE

   The message in this book stresses that God loves you and wants you to experience His peace and life.

   The BIBLE says ... For God loved the world so much that He gave His only Son, so that everyone who believes in Him may not die but have eternal life. John 3:16

2. REALIZE OUR PROBLEM—SEPARATION

   People choose to disobey God and go their own way. This results in separation from God.

   The BIBLE says ... Everyone has sinned and is far away from God's saving presence. Romans 3:23

3. RESPOND TO GOD'S REMEDY—CROSS OF CHRIST

   God sent His Son to bridge the gap. Christ did this by paying the penalty of our sins when He died on the cross and rose from the grave.

   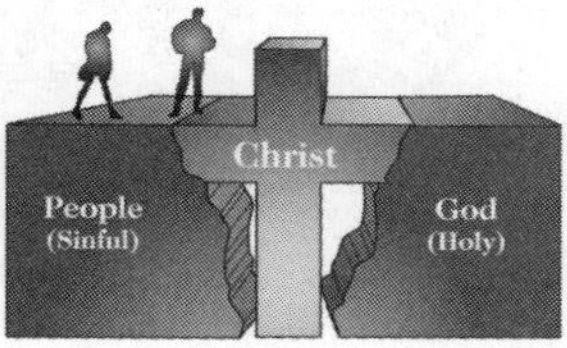

   The BIBLE says ... But God has shown us how much He loves us—it was while we were still sinners that Christ died for us! Romans 5:8

4. RECEIVE GOD'S SON—LORD AND SAVIOR

   You cross the bridge into God's family when you ask Christ to come into your life.

   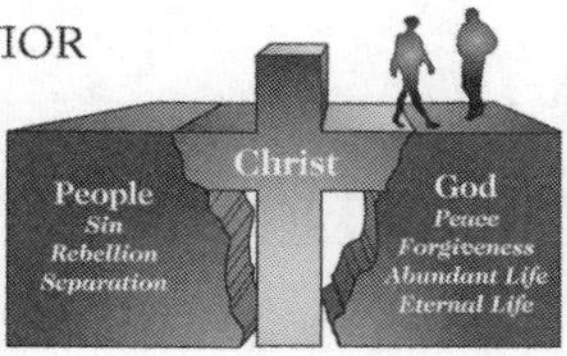

   The BIBLE says ... Some, however, did receive Him and believed in Him; so He gave them the right to become God's children. John 1:12

THE INVITATION IS TO:

REPENT (turn from your sins) and by faith RECEIVE Jesus Christ into your heart and life and follow Him in obedience as your Lord and Savior.

PRAYER OF COMMITMENT

"Dear Lord Jesus, I know that I am a sinner, and I ask for Your forgiveness. I believe You died for my sins and rose from the dead. I turn from my sins and invite You to come into my heart and life. I want to trust and follow You as my Lord and Savior. In Your Name, Amen."

Sketch Artists

Left to right:

Stephen Henning—*Landscape Painter*

Krista Fearing—*Children's Book Illustrator*

Becky H. Tighe—*Visual, Graphic, Sculpture, Media*

Artists are members of Lake Region Arts Council
http://www.lrac4.org/artists/index.asp